Three Wise Women

Three Wise Women

40 Devotions
Celebrating Advent with
Mary, Elizabeth, and Anna

DANDI DALEY MACKALL

PARACLETE PRESS
Brewster, Massachusetts

2022 First Printing

Three Wise Women: 40 Devotions Celebrating Advent with Mary, Elizabeth, and Anna

Copyright © 2022 by Dandi Daley Mackall

ISBN 978-1-64060-805-4

The Paraclete Press name and logo are trademarks of Paraclete Press.

Library of Congress Cataloging-in-Publication Data
Names: Mackall, Dandi Daley, author.
Title: Three wise women : 40 devotions celebrating Advent with Mary,
   Elizabeth, and Anna / Dandi Daley MacKall.
Description: Brewster, Massachusetts : Paraclete Press, 2022. | Summary:
   "The struggles and joys of Mary, Elizabeth, and Anna should connect with
   what most readers experience at Christmas and perhaps, every day"--
   Provided by publisher.
Identifiers: LCCN 2022019678 (print) | LCCN 2022019679 (ebook) | ISBN
   9781640608054 (hardcover) | ISBN 9781640608061 (epub) | ISBN
   9781640608078 (pdf)
Subjects: LCSH: Advent--Meditations. | Mary, Blessed Virgin, Saint. |
   Elizabeth (Mother of John the Baptist), Saint. | Anna (Biblical
   prophetess) | BISAC: RELIGION / Holidays / Christmas & Advent | RELIGION
   / Biblical Meditations / New Testament
Classification: LCC BV40 .M336 2022 (print) | LCC BV40 (ebook) | DDC
   242/.33--dc23/eng/20220614
LC record available at https://lccn.loc.gov/2022019678
LC ebook record available at https://lccn.loc.gov/20220196

10 9 8 7 6 5 4 3 2 1

Published by Paraclete Press
Brewster, Massachusetts
www.paracletepress.com

Printed in Korea

To the wonderful women
who are my gifts from God:

DAUGHTERS
Jen, Katy, and Bri

GRANDDAUGHTERS
Ellie, Cassie, Madison, and Harper

SISTERS
My sister, Maureen; sisters-in-law, Mary and Ann;
Laurie, and so many sisters in Christ

CONTENTS

AUTHOR'S NOTE

*But Mary treasured all these words
and pondered them in her heart.*

(Luke 2:19)

How we need to ponder the miracle of Christ's birth!

We've heard about the famed *Three Wise Men*, but what about the *Three Wise Women*? At the center of the First Christmas events were three very wise women: Mary (Jesus' mother), Elizabeth (mother of John the Baptist), and Anna the Prophetess (who served in the temple most of her adult life, waiting, expecting, to see the Messiah). My hope is that you'll identify with these women, pondering the Scriptures, then imaging what Mary, Elizabeth, and Anna may have been going through around the time our Savior was born.

We don't get many detailed thoughts from the three wise women as the world around them changed forever, but we do read their amazing, true stories in the Scriptures. The Bible's account is what you can depend on and understand as absolute truth, so I have included many of the passages and references for ease and study.

My imagined thoughts in these pages are based on what the Scriptures reveal about Mary, Elizabeth, and Anna. I've tried *never* to let their imagined voices stray from what we *are* given in the Bible. Before each day's devotional, I've included the scriptural accounts and relevant verses, which we can trust and consider. I've studied the culture for context and prayerfully attempted to get inside the heads of these wonderful women in an effort to deeply connect with them and their society. I invite you to do the same.

Study the Scriptures for yourself this Advent season and see what the Bible reveals to us about Mary, Elizabeth, and Anna. Imagine their joys and struggles from different perspectives. Keep in mind: They were women. They were believers in an Almighty God. And they were flesh-and-blood real.

As Christmas approaches, I invite you to meditate on the contributions of these women. In the midst of what can turn into Christmas craziness, find a quiet spot where you can listen to the voices of Mary, Elizabeth, and Anna. As you read about them, walk in their sandals, see their Middle Eastern landscapes, and hear their hopes and dreams as they wait for the coming Messiah. Let yourself be drawn deeper into the heart of God this season as you identify with the Wise Women and share with them the miracle of Christmas.

How amazing are the deeds of the LORD!
All who delight in him should ponder them.

(Psalm 111:2, NLT)

MARY
of Nazareth

In the sixth month the angel Gabriel
was sent by God to a town in Galilee called
Nazareth, to a virgin engaged to a man whose
name was Joseph, of the house of David.
The virgin's name was Mary.

(Luke 1:26–27)

God could have sent his Son fully grown, the way he created the first man, Adam. Yet God chose to enter our world as a baby, nestled inside Mary's womb for nine months.

The greatest news in all the world might have been delivered first to kings and nobles with trumpets blaring. But the announcement came to Mary, a young girl, common and unmarried, a virgin.

The birth of the Savior could have occurred in Herod's grand palace of gold and marble, or in the temple of Jerusalem, the aroma of incense blessing the air. But it was Mary who carried God's Son in the dark silence of her womb, and Mary who gave birth to the hope of the world. As she wrapped her baby in strips of cloth, the smell of hay, donkey sweat, and dung wafted over the manger.

Religious leaders, trained to understand revelations, might have explained and interpreted the birth of the Messiah with words clear and filled with learning. But Mary listened to the shepherds, whose words tumbled from them like sheep trampling over one another.

What might Mary have been thinking throughout the greatest event of all time?

MARY

DECEMBER 1

Hope

And so, Lord, where do I put my hope?
My only hope is in you.
(Psalm 39:7, NLT)

●

Let us hold fast to the confession of our hope without
wavering, for he who has promised is faithful.
(Hebrews 10:23)

●

Why are you cast down, O my soul, and why are you
disquieted within me? Hope in God; for I shall again
praise him, my help and my God.
(Psalm 42:11)

●

For you, O Lord, are my hope, my trust,
O LORD, from my youth.
(Psalm 71:5)

●

But this I call to mind,
and therefore I have hope:
The steadfast love of the LORD never ceases,
his mercies never come to an end.

(Lamentations 3:21–22)

●

Hope

Such a God we have! I climbed the hill behind our house this morning until I could see the Plains of Megiddo below Nazareth. Fields of barley and wheat begin to sprout beyond the valley, filling the air with earthly scents. I love all of Galilee. It's true that I have not traveled far from my little village. For a half-century, we and all of Palestine have been ruled by Rome.

But I hope for nothing more than to live here, among heavy-laden olive trees, tall sycamores, and ancient pines, perhaps with a good man like Joseph. I am eligible for betrothal, having passed the age of twelve years and a day.

On my return home, I walked by the workplace of Joseph's father. His mother spoke kindly to me, offering the blessing of the day. I heard chisels and hammers from within the shop. Because of the brightness of the sun, I could only make out two shadowy figures at work—Joseph and his father, no doubt.

I hope Joseph might speak to his father, and then to mine. But perhaps it is only my own longing that makes me imagine Joseph looks on me with favor.

My hope, O Lord, is in You.

PONDERING . . .

1. What did you hope for years ago? Where do you think your hope(s) originated? Did your hopes come true?

2. Think about one of your hopes that was never fulfilled. How do you think your life might have turned out differently if that hope had been granted? No one knows, except God. In retrospect, can you see a hint of God's thoughts, which are higher than ours?

3. Name three things you're hoping for this Christmas. How disappointed will you be if you don't receive any of them?

4. What do you think it means to "hope in the Lord"? Is there anything you can do this Advent to strengthen your hope in the Lord?

Dear God,
My hope is in you alone.

MARY

DECEMBER 2

Waiting

I wait for the LORD, my whole being waits,
and in his word I put my hope.
(Psalm 130:5, NIV)

•

I believe that I shall see the goodness of the LORD
in the land of the living.
Wait for the LORD; be strong,
and let your heart take courage;
wait for the LORD!
(Psalm 27:13–14)

•

And it will be said on that day,
"Behold, this is our God for whom we have waited
that He might save us. This is the LORD for whom
we have waited;
Let's rejoice and be glad in His salvation."
(Isaiah 25:9, NASB)

•

Waiting

I have passed another day fulfilling my daily duties, sweeping, squeezing the oils and making butter, helping prepare meals, and fetching water. At the well, it is tempting to listen to idle talk. For most young girls in this village, their talk always seems to return to betrothal and wedding ceremonies, though we have very little say in the matter. As for me, my thoughts, not my speech, fly to Joseph. I have heard nothing from Joseph, or from my father.

Now, as a breeze stirs the leaves around me, I must gather the few acacia sticks that remain behind our house. I turn my thoughts to God, and my Creator fills me with his presence. I gaze in wonder at his handiwork—a twisted tree trunk, the sun sinking through pink and purple clouds that swirl against the blue sky above Nazareth.

Once, my parents took me to the hill country of Judea, where our relatives, Elizabeth and Zechariah the Priest, live. We had been walking for days when I stumbled on the rocky ground of what I imagined a never-ending desert.

Then suddenly, as if in a vision, I looked up from the rocks and dust, and there she was—Jerusalem, the city of our forefathers. We did not enter, but watched as travelers poured through the city gate.

I would not want to live in Jerusalem, though I would enjoy visiting there.

Perhaps if the Lord blesses, Joseph and I will take our firstborn son to the Jerusalem temple for dedication.

"Mary? Mary!" Mother calls me from my daydreams. "The wood will not collect itself, and the night falls fast."

"I'm sorry, Mother," I say, gathering the sticks at my feet.

She is right, of course.

I wait, and I pray to Adonai, the One who rules in mighty power, that his will be done. My future is in his hands alone.

PONDERING . . .

1. Where does your mind go when you daydream? What does that tell you about yourself?

2. Is there a longtime prayer you're still waiting to be answered yes? Why do you think you've had to wait?

3. What do you do when you're waiting for the answer to an urgent prayer? What do you do when you're waiting for weeks, or months, or years?

4. How do you know when God has answered, but the answer is "No"? Can you recall several examples and how you knew? Did this change your view of God or of yourself?

Dear God,
I will wait upon you.

MARY

DECEMBER 3

Love

Now in the sixth month the angel Gabriel was sent by
God to a city of Galilee named Nazareth, to a virgin
betrothed to a man whose name was Joseph,
of the house of David.
The virgin's name was Mary.
(Luke 1:26–27, NKJV)

●

Like the finest apple tree in the orchard
is my lover among other young men. . . .
He escorts me to the banquet hall;
it's obvious how much he loves me.
(Song of Solomon 2:3–4, NLT)

●

Love is patient, love is kind. It does not envy, it does
not boast, it is not proud. It does not dishonor others,
it is not self-seeking, it is not easily angered,
it keeps no record of wrongs. Love does not delight in
evil but rejoices with the truth.
It always protects, always trusts,
always hopes, always perseveres.
(1 Corinthians 13:4–7, NIV)

•

And now faith, hope, and love abide,
these three; and the greatest of these is love.
(1 Corinthians 13:13)

•

If I speak in the tongues of men or of angels, but
do not have love, I am only a resounding gong or a
clanging cymbal. If I have the gift of prophecy
and can fathom all mysteries and
all knowledge, and if I have a faith that can move
mountains, but do not have love, I am nothing. If
I give all I possess to the poor and give over my
body to hardship that I may boast,
but do not have love, I gain nothing.
(1 Corinthians 13:1–3, NIV)

•

Love

If I were a lion, I would roar for joy until all Nazareth quaked. If I were a mourning dove, I would fly high above the white cloud wisps and sing out my gladness and praise.

Joseph of Nazareth, an honest craftsman like his father, will be my betrothed. For this I have waited, and the Lord has given me the finest man in all Galilee. My father arranged our marriage, and I do not know if he or my mother knew my heart.

The betrothal feast is only weeks away, and then Joseph and I shall be legally bound to marry, as if I would need the law to keep me pledged to such a man as Joseph of Nazareth, a descendant of King David himself. I have already begun imagining the home my betrothed will make for us after our betrothal ceremony. Every bridegroom must do so for his bride, but not every husband is a carpenter. It is our tradition that the bridegroom will add three walls and a roof to his father's house, a construction Joseph may complete when not building houses and furnishings for others. I care not. I would be content to live in a livestock shelter as long as I have Joseph alongside me.

Such happiness—could this be a dream?

• • •

It was a simple, beautiful, ceremony. Joseph and I are betrothed. At the feast, Joseph gave me a necklace of fine stone and carving. As he placed it around my neck, he looked directly into my eyes—such deep, brown eyes my betrothed has, as if God's Spirit shines through him from his soul.

"See by this token," he said, his voice strong as thunder, yet gentle as the rolling stream. "Thou art set apart for me, according to the law of Moses and of Israel."

It is how I feel—set apart for my betrothed. Joseph has pledged carpenter tools and fine dinner plates to my father for the mohar. In exchange, my father has given my dowry. It is meager, yet Joseph acts as though he has received a palace.

Our God has blessed me with a woman's love for this man, a longing I have never felt. When Joseph left for his home, my heart wanted to follow.

PONDERING . . .

1. Who are the people in your life who most deserve your deepest love? How would you define your love for each person? How would you describe your love for God?

2. The Apostle John wrote to believers: "Beloved, if God so loved us, we also ought to love one another" (1 John 4:11, NASB). What does God's love have to do with your expression of loving others? Is there anyone you have trouble loving?

3. How can you express your love this Advent season—to those you already love, and to those you're having trouble liking?

4. Why do you think 1 Corinthians 13 says that love is even greater than hope and faith?

Dear God,
Thank you for your unfailing love.

MARY

DECEMBER 4

True Affection

Let love be genuine; hate what is evil,
hold fast to what is good; love one another with
mutual affection; outdo one another in showing honor.
(Romans 12:9–10)

●

Let your wife be a fountain of blessing for you.
Rejoice in the wife of your youth.
(Proverbs 5:18, NLT)

●

He who finds a wife finds a good thing, and
obtains favor from the LORD.
(Proverbs 18:22)

·

For this very reason, you must make every effort
to support your faith with goodness, and goodness
with knowledge, and knowledge with self-control,
and self-control with endurance, and endurance
with godliness, and godliness with mutual
affection, and mutual affection with love.
(2 Peter 1:5–7)

·

True Affection

Although my wedding is a full year away, Mother busies herself planning my wedding clothes. She embroiders until the sun hangs low in the sky. As for me, I would marry my Joseph in the robe I am wearing now.

Yet I do look forward to my wedding under the canopy, with our families gathered to share our joy. "Tell me more about the ceremony, Mother." I have attended many ceremonies, which last five or six or even seven days. Most follow the traditions and celebrate with friends and villagers, who come to feast and dance.

Mother does not look up from her needlework. "Joseph, too, shall wear his finest at the first evening of the celebration, and perhaps a crown. You will be carried in a litter during the procession, accompanied by our traditional songs. Have you spoken with your bridesmaids, Mary? You must talk to a dozen, though you will settle on ten."

I shake my head, for every moment, it is Joseph I wish to talk with.

• • •

"Compared to Father's usual customers, the Roman soldiers seem to require twice as much of everything," Joseph says, as we walk in the evening cool. "Although they are seldom pleasant to work for, they pay well enough that I can save for our home."

Our home. How I am growing to appreciate this godly man! Last evening Joseph and I observed an eagle that flew high above us. Joseph recited, "But those who wait for the LORD shall renew their strength. They shall mount up with wings like eagles!" (Isaiah 40:31a).

I believe our love is growing under the wings of our Lord. Now when Joseph looks at me, I can sense his love and deep affection. Has anyone ever felt such joy?

PONDERING . . .

1. Is there a difference between affection and love? Is it possible to have true love without affection?

2. In Mary's day, betrothals and weddings were strong commitments. In what ways have marriages and engagements changed? What do you see as the purpose of an engagement?

3. Has your affection for a loved one changed over the years? How and why?

4. How does your love for one another, and for God, grow? What do you do to help your love grow?

Dear God,
Bless my home
with love and affection.

MARY

DECEMBER 5

Restlessness

"For my thoughts are not your thoughts,
nor are your ways my ways," says the Lord.
"For as the heavens are higher than the earth,
so are my ways higher than your ways
and my thoughts than your thoughts."
(Isaiah 55:8–9)

•

Not that I am referring to being in need;
for I have learned to be content with whatever I have.
(Philippians 4:11)

•

Then I heard the voice of the Lord saying,
"Whom shall I send, and who will go for us?"
And I said, "Here am I; send me!"
(Isaiah 6:8)

•

And now the Lord says—
he who formed me in the womb to be his servant
to bring Jacob back to him
and gather Israel to himself,
for I am honored in the eyes of the Lord
and my God has been my strength
—he says:
"It is too small a thing for you to be my servant to
restore the tribes of Jacob
and bring back those of Israel I have kept.
I will also make you a light for the Gentiles, that
my salvation may reach to the ends of the earth."
(Isaiah 49:5–6, NIV)

•

Restlessness

Today I have climbed from the valley of Nazareth, beyond the cluster of dwellings, to the highest hills. From here, I can see across to Mount Carmel in the west, to the Jordan valley and the hills of Gilead to the east. Farther north lies Mount Hermon, snow-capped and majestic. South, below the foothills, through olive groves and vineyards, bands of people journey on the main route between Caesarea and Damascus.

At times, I cannot help but wonder what happens to these people who travel the roadway to the great cities beyond Jerusalem. Will they ever know Yahweh and his plan for their lives? What do they understand of the coming Messiah?

Mother says I think too much. She calls what I am feeling "wedding restlessness." I'm certain she, in her wisdom, must be right.

I love Joseph more with each passing day and want only our life together. Indeed, that has not changed. Joseph is my husband, and I his betrothed wife. Becoming a wife and mother is all I have ever dreamed of . . . and yet in my deepest soul, I feel there is something more—much, much more that God has for me to do.

Is this foolishness? Wedding restlessness? What more could any woman be called to do but to love and care for a good husband and to be blessed with many children?

PONDERING . . .

1. Have you ever felt restless, yet content with your life? What do you think causes this kind of restlessness?

2. How is a God-induced restlessness different from your own dissatisfaction with life? How can you tell the difference?

3. Queen Esther was called to risk her life in order to save her people. Her uncle Mordecai challenged her hesitation, asking, ". . . And who knows but that you have come to your royal position for such a time as this?" (Esther 4:14, NIV). Is there a possibility that God may be calling you to do something more, something out of your comfort zone?

4. What specific steps could you take to meet the challenge of God's calling?

Dear God,
Help my thoughts align with your will.

ELIZABETH
Mother *of* John the Baptist

In the days of King Herod of Judea, there was
a priest named Zechariah, who belonged
to the priestly order of Abijah. His wife was
a descendant of Aaron, and her name was
Elizabeth. Both of them were righteous before
God, living blamelessly according to all the
commandments and regulations of the Lord.
But they had no children, because Elizabeth was
barren, and both were getting on in years.

(Luke 1:5–7)

Elizabeth definitely qualifies as a wise woman. When Luke began his account of Jesus, he began with Elizabeth and Zechariah, a priestly couple living in the Judean hill country close to Jerusalem. The Roman Empire dominated the nation, and Herod ruled as king over Judea, but priests like Zechariah kept the Jewish religion and faith alive.

Elizabeth descended from the priestly line of Aaron, and as the wife of a priest, she would have been an important and respected woman in the Jewish community, except for one fact: She had no children, and now she was too old to give her husband sons and daughters. Barren women were considered cursed by God since children were not a choice, but an inheritance.

Elizabeth's husband served in the Temple of Jerusalem as one of an estimated 20,000 priests, who were divided into twenty-four groups to carry out temple duties. Zechariah's Abijah division was on duty when lots were cast to see who would enter the Holy Place to burn incense at the altar. The lot fell to Zechariah, and Elizabeth's life would be changed for all eternity.

ELIZABETH

DECEMBER 6

Loneliness

I lie awake; I am like a lonely bird
on the housetop.
(Psalm 102:7)

•

Turn to me and be gracious to me,
for I am lonely and afflicted.
(Psalm 25:16, NIV)

•

"And the one who sent me is with me;
he has not left me alone, for I always do what is
pleasing to him."
(John 8:29)

•

O Lord, all my longing is known to you; my
sighing is not hidden from you.
(Psalm 38:9)

•

Loneliness

Today I recline alone in the house and mend Zechariah's priestly robe. I wonder how my husband fares in Jerusalem. I wish I were there with him though this week.

As a member of the order of Abijah, my husband takes his turn serving in the Temple of Jerusalem. This year his division was appointed to serve on the Day of Atonement. Lots are drawn as God's way of selecting one priest to enter the holy sanctuary of the Lord and offer incense.

What if the lot falls to Zechariah? I can only imagine what it might feel like to enter the Holy Place, with its seven-branched candlestick, a golden altar on which to burn incense, and a table where shewbread is placed. What an honor that would be, to experience God's presence in such a way! These idle imaginings are not new to me, though I think of these matters with no envy or jealousy, only amazement. I continue to pray for the will of Adonai, our Lord and Master, and I thank him for his manifold blessings to us.

Zechariah should be entering the great temple courts at this very moment. I have stood in the Court of Women and attended many ceremonies there. As I have given praise to the Almighty, my heart always goes out to those lingering in the Court of the Gentiles. Foreigners and Gentiles are not allowed to pass through the Beautiful

Gate into the Court of Women. True, many come to trade commodities, exchange foreign money, or buy and sell sacrificial animals. Others come to worship. I know our Creator loves them all.

Now as I recline on my dining mat, resting, the calming aroma of freshly baked bread revives my senses. I must finish my chores. So much dust everywhere, like specks of sin covering the world.

Here in our home there is no sound but the stillness, no noise but what I, myself, make.

If the Almighty had honored us with children, I would not feel this loneliness when Zechariah leaves for Jerusalem. But I thank my Lord for the comfort of his presence.

PONDERING . . .

1. The psalmist David asked God, "Turn to me and be gracious to me, for I am lonely and afflicted" (Psalm 25:16). Do you ever feel lonely or left out? How do you handle loneliness? Do you tell anyone or keep it to yourself?

2. How often during the days of Advent are you aware of Christ's presence? How could you tune in more often? Even a quick prayer, such as "Thank you, Jesus," uttered in grateful praise throughout the day, can serve as a reminder that you're not really alone.

3. Have you had a long-term sorrow or disappointment, such as Elizabeth's childlessness? How did God answer your prayers? How has God helped you through it?

4. Elizabeth must have longed for a child. What do you long for? Why is this your longing? How can you know whether or not your longing is from God?

Dear God, Thank you for being "Immanuel," God with Us.

ELIZABETH

DECEMBER 7

Promises

One day Zechariah was serving God in the temple, for his order was on duty that week. As was the custom of the priests, he was chosen by lot to enter the sanctuary of the Lord and burn incense. While the incense was being burned, a great crowd stood outside, praying.

While Zechariah was in the sanctuary, an angel of the Lord appeared to him, standing to the right of the incense altar. Zechariah was shaken and overwhelmed with fear when he saw him. But the angel said, "Don't be afraid, Zechariah! God has heard your prayer. Your wife, Elizabeth, will give you a son, and you are to name him John. You will have great joy and gladness, and many will rejoice at his birth, for he will be great in the eyes of the Lord. He must never touch wine or other alcoholic drinks. He will be filled with the Holy Spirit, even before his birth. And he will turn many Israelites to the Lord their God. He will be a man with the spirit and power of Elijah. He will prepare the people for the coming of the Lord. He will turn the hearts of the fathers to their children, and he will cause those who are rebellious to accept the wisdom of the godly."

Zechariah said to the angel, "How can I be sure this will happen? I'm an old man now, and my wife is also well along in years."

Then the angel said, "I am Gabriel! I stand in the very presence of God. It was he who sent me to bring you this good news! But now, since you didn't believe what I said, you will be silent and unable to speak until the child is born. For my words will certainly be fulfilled at the proper time."

(Luke 1:8–20, NLT)

•

Promises

I am afraid to write what happened yesterday, fearful it may turn out to be a dream, like so many other dreams I have awoken from over the past thirty years.

But there sits my husband, watching me from across the room as if I am more precious than gold. I feel like a child, yet more like a woman than I ever dared.

I knew when I saw Zechariah's head bob over the crest of the hill, something was wrong. He was trotting, stumbling, then running like a young man half his age.

I wiped my hands on my apron, closed the lid on the oven fires, and stood in the doorway, squinting against the afternoon sun. "What is it, husband?" I cried.

Zechariah ran to me and threw his arms around me, lifting me off my feet as he used to do when we were betrothed. But he did not speak.

"Something has happened?" I asked, pressing my hands against his chest and looking into his timeworn face.

Still, he said nothing, though he nodded vigorously.

"Why do you not speak, Zechariah?"

He rolled his eyes and grinned.

Believing he had taken ill, I pulled him to sit beside me on the rug I crafted years ago.

Still holding my hand, he pulled me to sit on his lap. I felt a rush of warmth—embarrassed at my age by my husband of so many years.

Then Zechariah threw his arms in the air between us. Like flying birds, his hands flapped and darted soundlessly.

"I don't understand," I said.

He kissed me, and when he drew away, he had tears dancing in his eyes, running down his cheeks, getting lost in his beard. My husband pressed the flat of his hand against my belly, held me with an intent gaze, and slowly nodded. Up and down. Up and down.

And I knew.

I will bear him a son.

PONDERING . . .

1. What's the best news you've ever received? How did you react? What details can you recall?

2. Why do you think Elizabeth had to wait so long for a child? Why do you think God doesn't always answer instantly?

3. What promises has God made to you? Which promises have you seen fulfilled, and which ones haven't been (yet)? Do you believe all of God's promises will come true?

4. Zechariah wanted a sign to reassure him that the angel's announcement would come true. Why do you think Elizabeth did not ask for a sign?

Dear God,
Fulfill your promises in my life.
Open my eyes to your plan.

ELIZABETH

DECEMBER 8

Grace

After those days his wife Elizabeth conceived, and
for five months she remained in seclusion. She
said, "This is what the Lord has done for me when
he looked favorably on me and took away the
disgrace I have endured among my people."
(Luke 1:24–25)

·

For the LORD God is a sun and shield;
he bestows favor and honor.
No good thing does the LORD withhold
from those who walk uprightly.
(Psalm 84:11)

·

He gives the barren woman a home,
making her the joyous mother of children.
Praise the Lord!
(Psalm 113:9)

•

Behold, children are a gift of the Lord,
The fruit of the womb is a reward.
(Psalm 127:3, NASB)

•

Grace

I am filled with gratitude to Elohim, the one and only God, full of power and might, for he has taken away my shame. How many years have women referred to me as *Elizabeth the Barren One*? How many times have I avoided gatherings at the well when news erupted that another woman was with child?

I have rejoiced with other women as they shared delight in their children, God's richest blessings. I admit a certain pain has accompanied my shared joy, a sting when someone younger speaks of another grandchild, then eyes me with pity, or condemnation.

But now I, *The Barren One,* am barren no more.

I do not want word of my blessing to spread by well-gossip, as is our custom in the hills. So I have decided to stay at home in seclusion. True, part of me wants my neighbors to notice my swollen belly. But I easily resist my fleeting temptation. This child is God's gift to me, by his grace. A gift comes at the sole discretion and lovingkindness of the Giver. I have done nothing to earn such a treasure. The Lord has done this for me.

I will savor every moment, the wonder of this life inside me. I will share it with no one but my husband . . . and my Lord.

PONDERING . . .

1. Is there anything that causes you pain because you haven't been given the same gift as someone else? How has that pain or desire affected your relationship with others? With God?

2. Can you identify gifts that you do have that many don't? Do you think their envy causes them pain? What might you do when you realize someone wishes they had what you have?

3. Jesus' coming to earth is about grace and forgiveness. This Christmas, consider how you can offer grace to others. Is there someone you should forgive?

4. How would you define "grace"? What evidence of grace do you see in your own life?

Dear God,
Thank you for your grace in my life and for
all your gifts.

ELIZABETH

DECEMBER 9

Worry

"Therefore I tell you, do not worry about your life, what you will eat or drink; or about your body, what you will wear. Is not life more than food, and the body more than clothes? Look at the birds of the air; they do not sow or reap or store away in barns, and yet your heavenly Father feeds them. Are you not much more valuable than they? Can any one of you by worrying add a single hour to your life?

"And why do you worry about clothes? See how the flowers of the field grow. They do not labor or spin. Yet I tell you that not even Solomon in all his splendor was dressed like one of these. If that is how God clothes the grass of the field, which is here today and tomorrow is thrown into the fire, will he not much more clothe you—you of little faith? So do not worry, saying, 'What shall we eat?' or 'What shall we drink?' or 'What shall we wear?' For the pagans run after all these things, and your heavenly Father knows that you need them.

"But seek first his kingdom and his righteousness, and all these things will be given to you as well. Therefore do not worry about tomorrow, for tomorrow will worry about itself. Each day has enough trouble of its own."

(Matthew 6:25–34, NIV)

•

"Come to me, all you who are weary and burdened, and I will give you rest. Take my yoke upon you and learn from me, for I am gentle and humble in heart, and you will find rest for your souls. For my yoke is easy and my burden is light."

(Matthew 11:28–30, NIV)

•

Worry

My blessing grows inside me. I admit it has not always been easy to enjoy the nausea and changes of the past weeks. My back aches with the extra weight I carry. What will it be in months to come?

Though Zechariah and I do not discuss such concerns—he still cannot speak—I wonder if I will be too old to raise a son. Will I have the strength to carry my baby to temple? Will I have the stamina to chase after my child as he advances in age? Will my mind remain clear and my faith strong enough to raise our son in the love of God and belief in his promises?

My husband is older still. What if he never regains his powers of speech? Can he still serve in the temple? Will he be too old to teach the ways of manhood to our boy?

What if God were to take Zechariah and leave me here, alone?

But I will never be alone. And God will never fail or forsake me.

Forgive me my anxious thoughts, O Giver of all Good Gifts. For you alone are able. You created the heavens and earth and everything on the earth, in the skies, and under the seas. You breathe life into humans; and without you, there would be no life. It was you, Adonai, who brought your people out of slavery in Egypt, you who parted the Red Sea for them to walk through.

You knew us, and loved us, before the world began, and you always carry out your plans. Nothing is impossible for you. Not one thing is even difficult! You have given me my son, a gift and a miracle. This you did for Sarah and Abraham, giving them a child in their old age and descendants as numerous as the stars in the sky. We have seen miracle after miracle.

O Lord, I know you would not have called me to a task for which you would not prepare and sustain me. Help me trust you every moment, waving away unworthy thoughts of the future. I know you hold all things in your hands.

PONDERING . . .

1. List three things you're worried about today. Number them in order of the time spent worrying about them. Bring each worry before God. What steps can you take to increase your trust in God?

2. List five worries you've had in the past. How many of those worries actually materialized? In Matthew 6:34, Jesus says each day has enough trouble of its own. What did he mean by that?

3. What's the best way to handle worries and anxious thoughts? Give an example of a time when you handled a worry effectively.

4. Jesus says to take his yoke and he will give you rest. What could that mean in practical terms between now and Christmas Day?

Dear God,
I give you every anxious thought and ask
that your strength fill my being.

ELIZABETH

DECEMBER 10

Wonder

In those days John the Baptist appeared in the
wilderness of Judea, proclaiming,
"Repent, for the kingdom of heaven has come near."
This is the one of whom the prophet Isaiah spoke
when he said,
"The voice of one crying out in the wilderness:
'Prepare the way of the Lord,
make his paths straight.'"
(Matthew 3:1–3)

•

A voice cries out:
"In the wilderness prepare the way of the Lord,
make straight in the desert a highway for our God.
Every valley shall be lifted up,
and every mountain and hill be made low;
the uneven ground shall become level,
and the rough places a plain.
Then the glory of the Lord shall be revealed,
and all people shall see it together,
for the mouth of the Lord has spoken."
(Isaiah 40:3–5)

•

The whole earth is filled with awe at your wonders;
where morning dawns, where evening fades, you
call forth songs of joy.
(Psalm 65:8, NIV)

•

Wonder

Zechariah has made known to me a further message given by the angel in the Holy Place. Our son will prepare the way for the Lord's anointed, the Messiah of God! Such an honor fills me with wonder at the Lord's lovingkindness and is almost too great to bear. Our son may have a place among the great prophets of old!

We have gone so long without a prophet in Israel. And the last one, Malachi, prophesied about our John, the "Elijah" who would turn the hearts of fathers to their children, and the children's hearts to their fathers, preparing them for the Messiah.

I find myself wondering who the mother of the anointed is to be. Will our son be old when the Messiah does come? Or could they be the same age? That would mean the virgin is with child at this moment. But who?

When I was a young girl, I used to dream of being the virgin spoken of by Isaiah. I know many young girls shared that dream. Then I married Zechariah—a wonderful match, son of a priest, a righteous man. We have had a good life. And now my only disgrace has been taken away. We will have a son.

Still I wonder.

Is a young girl carrying the Savior at this very moment?

The birth is to be in Bethlehem of Judea, so the Scriptures tell us. Perhaps the virgin lives there. We know few families in Bethlehem, but—

I must stop. How can I try to imagine the plans of the Almighty? Praise be to God for his mighty secrets and wonders!

PONDERING . . .

1. Why do you think God keeps secrets from us? What would you like to know about the future?

2. How would you define a prophet? What do you know about the Old Testament prophets?

3. A study of Old Testament times suggests that many young women likely dreamed of being chosen mother of the Messiah. Would you have hoped to be chosen? Explain.

4. What do you know about the Messiah prophesied in the Bible? What do you think most people in Israel were expecting? What are some of your expectations for the rest of your life on earth?

Dear God,
Open my eyes and my heart as you reveal
your glory throughout this day.

ANNA
the Prophetess

There was also a prophet, Anna the daughter of Phanuel, of the tribe of Asher. She was of a great age, having lived with her husband seven years after her marriage, then as a widow to the age of eighty-four. She never left the temple but worshiped there with fasting and prayer night and day. At that moment she came, and began to praise God and to speak about the child to all who were looking for the redemption of Jerusalem.

(Luke 2:36–38)

•

One who dwells in the shelter of the Most High Will lodge in the shadow of the Almighty.

(Psalm 91:1, NASB)

•

Although her story in Scripture is told in only three verses, Anna the Prophetess delivers a powerful message of faithfulness and faith in El Shaddai, the Mighty One, the One who provides shelter, refuge, and rest. Anna's father, Phanuel, came from the tribe of Asher, part of the northern kingdom of Israel lost to the Assyrians in 722 BC. It's a wonder that a woman from one of the "lost" tribes was found in the Temple of Jerusalem.

Anna had been married for seven years when her husband died. At the beginning of her story in Scripture, she was an 84-year-old widow. As a prophetess, Anna would have stayed in, or close to, the temple so she could be available for those who needed her. She may have had lodgings in the women's court of the temple or in an adjoining alms-house or apartment. She worshiped in the temple every day, praying and fasting, and talking about the coming Messiah, who would rescue his people. She readied the temple-goers for the coming redemption through God's Messiah.

ANNA

DECEMBER 11

Comfort

Sing to God, sing in praise to his name,
exalt him who rides upon the clouds.
Rejoice in the presence of this God
whose name is the Lord.
The Father of orphans and the
defender of widows:
such is God in his holy dwelling place.
(Psalm 68:5–6, NCB)

•

"Blessed are those who mourn,
for they will be comforted."
(Matthew 5:4)

•

Blessed *be* the God and Father of our Lord Jesus Christ, the Father of mercies and God of all comfort, who comforts us in all our affliction so that we will be able to comfort those who are in any affliction with the comfort with which we ourselves are comforted by God.
(2 Corinthians 1:3–4, NASB)

•

The LORD is near to the brokenhearted, and saves the crushed in spirit. (Psalm 34:18)

•

As a mother comforts her child, so I will comfort you; you shall be comforted in Jerusalem.
(Isaiah 66:13)

•

Comfort

Today as I prayed in the Outer Court of the Temple of Jerusalem, a young Israelite woman stood silently a short distance from me. I perceived by her downcast and reddened eyes that she was in need, and the Spirit encouraged me to speak with her.

It took little to elicit her story of a grief and disappointment I have experienced in my own life. I thanked the Lord for the comfort he has provided me for so many years, and I prayed our God would help me share that comfort.

We passed through the Court of the Gentiles into the Court of Women. "I am truly sorry for the loss of your young husband and for all that has befallen you since," I began. "You will always miss your beloved, but God loves you deeply, and he will take care of you."

When she gave no response, I prayed for the right words. "It's not easy for a woman, especially under the reign of King Herod. As widows, we become more dependent. Yet this dependence can open the door to the depth of God's presence as he provides in miraculous ways. My husband was taken from me after seven years of marriage. Since then, our gracious Elohim has been my husband. His Word is my delight and my guide."

She lifted her head, and I could see ancestral beauty in her broad forehead and high cheekbones. I continued. "God may lead you to another husband, and that is in his hands alone. If he does not, then I promise that our faithful Lord will be as a loving husband to you eternally. Jehovah-Jireh, *The Lord Provides*, will see to all of your needs as you trust in him."

She nodded, with the trace of a smile that faded like a half-moon retreating behind gray clouds. Before she left the Court of Women, the young woman placed a coin into the temple treasury, a sign, I hope, that she will not grasp money for her security, but only grasp the hand of Jehovah-Jireh.

PONDERING . . .

1. Have you suffered major grief in your life? How did you react? Did you eventually realize God's comfort? In what forms do you think comfort may come?

2. Think of three disappointments you have experienced. What was your first reaction to each? Did that response change over time? If you're disappointed or angry, talk it over with God. He won't disappoint. Let him comfort you.

3. Have you ever been comforted by someone who had gone through the same experience you were going through? How has God allowed you to comfort others?

4. How can God be your Father? Your Husband? Your Comforter? Your Jehovah-Jireh?

Dear God,
In you alone, I rejoice. Help me to comfort
others the way you comfort me.

ANNA

DECEMBER 12

Wise Waiting

Happy is the one who listens to me,
watching daily at my gates,
waiting beside my doors.
(Proverbs 8:34)

•

O Lord, in the morning you hear my voice;
in the morning I plead my case to you, and watch.
(Psalm 5:3)

•

My soul waits for the Lord more than watchmen
for the morning, more than watchmen
for the morning.
(Psalm 130:6, RSV)

•

And again Isaiah says,
"The root of Jesse shall come,
the one who rises to rule the Gentiles;
in him the Gentiles shall hope."
(Romans 15:12)

•

Wise Waiting

How lovely the sky covers us this morning, as if El-Shaddai-Rohi, the Almighty Creator of heaven and earth, has spent the night painting blues, pinks, and purples—just for one old woman, me!

I awoke this morning as I do most mornings, wondering aloud, "Dear Father, will you send the Messiah this day?" Because of God's promise to send us a Savior, the Messiah, from the root of Jesse, I am expectant, watching and waiting. We have so many assurances that the Messiah will come. As the Lord Almighty promised the prophet Malachi: *See, I am sending my messenger to prepare the way before me, and the Lord whom you seek will suddenly come to his temple. The messenger of the covenant in whom you delight—indeed, he is coming, says the LORD of hosts* (Malachi 3:1).

I will be here in the temple waiting.

I make myself available for counsel in the Court of Women. As I stand among throngs of people, the scents of sacrificed animals, burnt offerings, and incense make their way to me. It is as if I am surrounded by God's presence and leadership, as were the Israelites who followed Moses out of Egypt, guided with a cloud by day, and a pillar of fire by night. The Ark of the Covenant has been gone since the destruction of Solomon's Temple, but God is here.

Isaiah promised: *Therefore the Lord himself will give you a sign: The virgin will conceive and give birth to a son, and will call him Immanuel* (Isaiah 7:14, NIV). Until that day, I do not wait idly. From morning to night, I pray and fast. And I speak with the worshipers who are waiting for redemption and for our Savior, the Messiah. I am as excited about this message today as I was on the first day I understood God's promise.

PONDERING . . .

1. How do we know Jesus was the Messiah? Do you believe Jesus is coming again? Does it make a difference to you in the "real world"?

2. What's the biggest thing you've had to wait for? How did you pass the time before you received what you'd been waiting for? Or not?

3. Are you waiting for something now? Anna did all she could while she was in "God's waiting room." What more can you do as you wait?

4. Anna seems the kind of person whose faith grows stronger while waiting to see a promise fulfilled. When you first believed in Jesus, were you excited about it? Are you less enthusiastic now, or more eager? Jesus cautions us about losing our first love for him. What can you do if you find your first love weakening?

Dear God,
I am waiting, watching, and expecting the
Messiah to transform my life!

ANNA

DECEMBER 13

Unseen

Because we look not to the things that are
seen but to the things that are unseen; for
the things that are seen are transient, but the
things that are unseen are eternal.
(2 Corinthians 4:18, RSV)

•

But whenever you pray, go into your room and shut
the door and pray to your Father who is in secret;
and your Father who sees in secret will reward you.
(Matthew 6:6)

•

Now faith is the assurance of things hoped for,
the conviction of things not seen. Indeed, by
faith our ancestors received approval. By faith we
understand that the worlds were prepared by the
word of God, so that what is seen was made from
things that are not visible.
(Hebrews 11:1–3)

•

A week later his disciples were again in the house, and Thomas was with them. Although the doors were shut, Jesus came and stood among them and said, "Peace be with you." Then he said to Thomas, "Put your finger here and see my hands. Reach out your hand and put it in my side. Do not doubt but believe." Thomas answered him, "My Lord and my God!" Jesus said to him, "Have you believed because you have seen me? Blessed are those who have not seen and yet have come to believe."

(John 20:26–29)

•

Although you have not seen him, you love him; and even though you do not see him now, you believe in him and rejoice with an indescribable and glorious joy, for you are receiving the outcome of your faith, the salvation of your souls.

(1 Peter 1:8–9)

•

Unseen

Yesterday I walked past the blind man who sits by the side of the road and begs for alms, food, money, anything that will alleviate his suffering. I gave him the little I had, but since catching a glimpse of his blank and sightless eyes in the light of the moon, I have wondered how he lives without seeing a sunset, the face of a child, or the intricacies of a delicate white lily. Does he believe they even exist?

God has revealed himself to us in so many ways, often through our senses: the beauty of creation, the vastness of the blue sky by day, and the wonder of shining stars by night. I see God in the slender grass blade, a bowing field of flax, a single rose, or grapes on the vine, swaying junipers, the sun glistening on the lake. The sight of ravens or swallows migrating, darkening the sky, then changing direction as if directed by an unseen instrument—these blessings point me to a gracious God.

And yet, our all-seeing God remains unseen. I believe in the unseen Lord, the only true God. He is the object of my faith. Maybe in this, the blind man and I are guided to the Holy One in the same way, as were our ancestors. Noah had likely never seen rain, but he believed God's warning of a flood and built an ark according to God's direction. Abraham didn't know where he was going when God instructed him to leave his home and become a stranger in a strange land. But he believed God, whom he had never seen. His barren wife, Sarah, old as I and well past the age of childbearing, came to believe the unseen God, who promised that their descendants would be countless as the sand on the seashore and the stars in the sky.

Though I cannot see God, I have experienced him. He has comforted me with his presence. He provides for me each day. He loves me. Can anyone *see* love? Yet there is no stronger force in the world. I cannot hold joy or peace in my hand, but they are more real than the wrinkles on my face.

I cannot see my God. But, oh, how grateful I am that Jehovah-Rohi sees me!

I must talk with the blind man this day.

PONDERING . . .

1. Name five "unseen" things you believe in. How do you know they exist?

2. Paul wrote the Corinthians that they shouldn't focus on what's seen, but on what is unseen. Things we can see are temporary, but those unseen are eternal. Consider your possessions and other things in your life, and divide them into "eternal" or "temporary."

3. Jesus told "Doubting Thomas" to stop doubting. How is that possible? When are you most likely to have doubts? Be honest, and talk to God about your struggles.

4. What would you say to a friend who doubts the true Christmas story? The Virgin Birth? The Resurrection? How can you be ready with the right answers given in the right spirit?

Dear God,
Help me in my unbelief,
those times I question or doubt.

MARY

DECEMBER 14

Belief

In the sixth month [of Elizabeth's pregnancy] the
angel Gabriel was sent by God to a town in Galilee
called Nazareth, to a virgin engaged to a man
whose name was Joseph, of the house of David.
The virgin's name was Mary. And he came to her
and said, "Greetings, favored one!
The Lord is with you."
(Luke 1:26–28)

•

"Therefore the Lord Himself will give you a sign:
Behold, the virgin shall conceive and bear a Son,
and shall call His name Immanuel."
(Isaiah 7:14, NKJV)

•

"Blessed is she who has believed that the Lord
would fulfill his promises to her!"
(Luke 1:45, NIV)

•

Belief

I have no one to tell of this miracle, the unthinkable, unspeakable grace and majesty of our God. What other god would bow so low as to come to his maidservant?

Yesterday began as most days since my betrothal. Joseph cut stone with his father, and my father worked in the fields. I gathered olives, then ground them in the village for oil. In the afternoon, my mother and I worked together grinding barley after my second trip to the well. As we added fermented dough and kneaded the mixture, we chatted about my future wedding feast.

Later, when I was alone, the light of a thousand stars suddenly filled the space around me. So supernaturally bright was the light that I feared I would be struck dead; I knew that I must be in the presence of the Almighty, before whom no one can stand.

But a being, an angel dressed in white, said, "Greetings, favored woman! The Lord is with you!" As if the angel could read my heart, he said, "Don't be afraid, Mary, for you have found favor with God."

That alone would have been enough to fill me with joy for the rest of my days. God's angel knew me by name and announced that I, Mary of Nazareth, had found favor with God?

But the Messenger had only begun his announcement. "You will conceive and give birth to a son, and you will name him Jesus. He will be very great and will be called the Son of the Most High. The Lord God will give him the throne of his ancestor David. And he will reign over Israel forever; his Kingdom will never end!" (Luke 1:26–33, NLT).

Now, in the light of the rising sun, I wonder at my own foolishness. I did not ask "Why me?" or "How will my son rule a kingdom that never ends?"

Instead, I asked only one question: "How can this happen? I am a virgin."

I have never spoken of such things with my parents. Yet as frightful as this angelic being was, I felt he knew me to the depths of my soul and would not take offense.

The angel answered, "The Holy Spirit will come upon you, and the power of the Most High will overshadow you. So the baby will be holy, and he will be called the Son of God.

"What's more, your relative Elizabeth has become pregnant in her old age! People used to say she was barren, but she has conceived a son and is now in her sixth month. For nothing is impossible with God."

"I am the Lord's servant. May everything you have said about me come true" (Ref. Luke 1:34–38, NLT).

Then the angel was gone.

Alone in the darkness, I felt a stillness so strong that the weight of it forced me to my knees.

PONDERING . . .

1. If you had been Mary of Nazareth, what do you think your reaction to Gabriel's message might have been? Which part of the announcement would have stood out to you? What would you have asked Gabriel?

2. What was it about Mary that made her God's choice as mother of Jesus? How do you know?

3. God honored Mary above all women. In what ways has God honored you?

4. Mary believed that nothing was impossible with God. Name three things you've been considering impossible. Is God big enough to handle the impossible?

Dear God,
I accept that nothing is impossible with you.
Help me to act on that belief.

MARY

DECEMBER 15

Alone

Then Mary said, "Here am I, the servant of the
Lord; let it be with me according to your word."
Then the angel departed from her.
(Luke 1:38)

•

Whom have I in heaven but you?
And there is nothing on earth that I desire
other than you.
(Psalm 73:25)

•

He alone is my rock and my salvation,
my fortress; I shall never be shaken.
(Psalm 62:2)

•

For God alone my soul waits in silence,
for my hope is from him.
(Psalm 62:5)

•

Alone

I must have fallen into a deep sleep after the angel left. During the night, I praised our mighty Jehovah for his grace to visit the lowly, to come to *me*.

I had to find Mother and share my joy with her. Surely the angel had visited my parents. I found her outside filling Father's breakfast cakes with olives. "Mother!"

"Bring in dried grass with the sticks this morning, Mary," she said, as if the world had not shifted.

"But we must talk," I said, confused by her disinterest.

"The fires will not make themselves," she said, not glancing my way.

I did as she asked, feeling insulated from the sounds of hooves passing, the cry of a baby in the next dwelling, and the clamor of tradesmen making their way to the marketplace.

Is it really possible they do not know?

• • •

I have fetched water each day, helped prepare meals, and obeyed my parents. Nothing has changed, but I know I am with child. Inside of me lives the Holy One of God, God's Son, who will save his people from their sin. How can I be so utterly transformed within, so completely set apart, when no one notices? Only Jehovah-Roi, "the God Who Sees."

The thought I keep pushing away is—What about my Joseph? He is unchanged, and to look at him pierces the depths of my soul. Joseph knows nothing of what God has done for his betrothed.

There is no one to talk to, except God alone.

PONDERING . . .

1. Consider your neighbors and others you have contact with at work, at church. Do you think anyone might be, or feel, alone this Christmas? What could you do to help?

2. Are you disappointed in anything or anyone this Christmas season? How would things change if you placed everything in God's hands and trusted him as Mary did?

3. Christmas can bring on sadness and depression, especially when we've lost people we love. How will this Christmas be different from other Christmases? Ponder the fact that God desires an intimate friendship with you. That's why he sent his Son, Jesus, Immanuel, God with Us.

4. What one specific change can you make in your life in order to draw closer to Christ by Christmas Day?

Dear God,
You are my rock and my salvation.
Help me to share this truth with others.

MARY

DECEMBER 16

Guidance

Trust in the LORD with all your heart,
and do not rely on your own insight.
In all your ways acknowledge him,
and he will make straight your paths.
(Proverbs 3:5–6)

•

Nevertheless I am continually with You;
You have taken hold of my right hand.
You will guide me with Your plan,
And afterward receive me to glory.
(Psalm 73:23–24, NASB)

•

He made my feet like the feet of a deer,
and set me secure on the heights.
(Psalm 18:33)

•

You gave me a wide place for my steps under me,
and my feet did not slip.
(Psalm 18:36)

Guidance

I can no longer go through days in Nazareth, where my mother continues to plan my wedding and Joseph gives candles to my parents for the Sabbath.

I am asking the God of All Wisdom to guide me through each day, and today my thoughts have turned to what the angel said of Elizabeth. No one here has heard of her miracle, but the angel told me she is with child. I long to see my dear relative and behold the promise God has made to her. How thankful I am for the Lord's guidance!

• • •

It is settled. Tomorrow I will go to the home of Elizabeth and Zechariah in the hill country of Judea. Mother wondered why I should visit our relatives at such a time, and I did not feel led to give her the reason. My God must have ruled in Mother's heart because she has agreed to my journey.

When I told Joseph of my plans, I read the pain in his dark eyes.

"Why do you leave?" he asked. And I heard the unspoken, "leave *me?*"

"I will come back." I forced a smile, but could say no more to him.

Father has secured a spot for me in a caravan, along with a young couple from Nazareth, who travel to the temple in Jerusalem to dedicate their firstborn child.

I do not know the way, but I know my Guide. He will protect me, and he will protect his Son.

PONDERING . . .

1. Think about at least three decisions you made in the past when you believed God was guiding you. How did you know?

2. Are you facing any decisions before the year ends? How is God guiding you? One name for God is "Yahweh-Rohi," "God is Our Shepherd." In what ways is God your Shepherd?

3. "Abba" is the most intimate name for God, as if we're calling our Father God "Daddy." What does it mean to you that the Almighty God chooses to be your "Daddy?"

4. How can we know if we're being guided by God, or by our own desires? What can we do to become more sensitive to God's guidance?

Dear God,
Guide me this day, Yahweh-Rohi,
my Shepherd.

MARY

DECEMBER 17

Friendship

In those days Mary set out and went with
haste to a Judean town in the hill country,
where she entered the house of Zechariah
and greeted Elizabeth.
(Luke 1:39–40)

•

Therefore encourage one another and build up
each other, as indeed you are doing.
(1 Thessalonians 5:11)

•

The heartfelt counsel of a friend is as sweet as
perfume and incense.
(Proverbs 27:9, NLT)

•

A friend loves at all times,
and kinsfolk are born to share adversity.
(Proverbs 17:17)

●

There are friends who pretend to be friends, but
there is a friend who sticks closer than a brother.
(Proverbs 18:24, RSV)

●

Friendship

Our little caravan took days, and I helped care for the children of my traveling companions. I wondered if they might grow up to know my Jesus. Each night, a canopy of bright stars reminded me that the Maker of Stars watches over me. The shape of the moon changed, diminished ever so slightly. But our God never changes, nor do his promises. And even the moon is full where we cannot see.

When we reached Jerusalem, I and my friends from Nazareth bid one another *shalom*. Then I walked the rocky path alone to Elizabeth's home, each step of the hill more difficult than the one before. My heart raced, but not with the strain. What, I wondered, would Elizabeth and Zechariah say when they saw me—they, who are blameless before God? What would they think if I told them I was with child?

I approached the door, touched the mezuzah of prayer, kissed my finger, and repeated the sacred words: "The Lord shall preserve thy going out and thy coming in from this time forth, and forever more."

Within, in the darkness of the house, a shadowed form grew closer—Zechariah, older than when last I had seen him. His eyes widened at the sight of me, but no words came from his open mouth. He stuck out his head and looked behind me, where I suppose he expected to see my father and mother.

When I turned from Zechariah and saw dear Elizabeth, her belly swollen with her blessing, my joy burst inside me. I had known in my heart Elizabeth would be with child—yes. But to see the belief in the flesh filled me with praise. "I greet you, dear Elizabeth," I cried, "with all the joy of our faithful God and Father!"

Elizabeth winced, wide-eyed, and started, as if pushed from within. Her fingers pressed against her belly. Such a radiance spread over her wrinkled face that the glow was that of an angel. "God has blessed you above all women, and your child is blessed."

With those words, I was no longer alone in my miracle. God had revealed himself to another woman. Elizabeth knew!

PONDERING . . .

1. Think about your best friends from childhood. What made your friendship strong? What hurt the friendship or let it fade?

2. Proverbs 18:24 talks about a friend who sticks closer than a brother. Do you have a friend who fits that description? Do you think that friend could be Jesus?

3. What characteristics of Elizabeth and Mary nurtured a deep friendship? How do you think they developed those characteristics and passed them to their children?

4. Consider your best friends now. How could you be a better friend? Is there one quality of Mary and Elizabeth's friendship, or Christ's friendship with you, that you could emulate and offer to a friend right now?

Dear God,
Help me be a friend and
an encouragement to others.

ELIZABETH

DECEMBER 18

Unselfish Joy

When Elizabeth heard Mary's greeting, the baby leaped in her womb, and Elizabeth was filled with the Holy Spirit. In a loud voice she exclaimed: "Blessed are you among women, and blessed is the child you will bear! But why am I so favored, that the mother of my Lord should come to me? As soon as the sound of your greeting reached my ears, the baby in my womb leaped for joy. Blessed is she who has believed that the Lord would fulfill his promises to her!"

(Luke 1:41–45, NIV)

•

It is good to give thanks to the Lord,
to sing praises to your name, O Most High;
to declare your steadfast love in the morning,
and your faithfulness by night,
to the music of the lute and the harp,
to the melody of the lyre.
For you, O Lord, have made me glad by your work;
at the works of your hands I sing for joy.
How great are your works, O Lord!
Your thoughts are very deep!
(Psalm 92:1–5)

●

Rejoice with those who rejoice,
weep with those who weep.
(Romans 12:15)

●

Unselfish Joy

Glory to God in the highest! Such a mighty Jehovah we have!

Yesterday as I busied myself with baking, I heard—no, I felt—someone at the doorway.

I wiped my hands and rose to follow Zechariah. Squinting at the entry, I could barely see as the hot sun burned behind the drape, blocking all but itself from my view. For a moment, I thought I saw a glow, as if from an angel. Then a small hand on the other side of the drape reached for the mezuzah on our doorpost, a symbol of our faith in God.

Zechariah crossed to the threshold. Intrigued, I followed after him as he pushed aside the drape.

There stood little Mary, my relative from Nazareth, layered in dust from covered head to sandaled foot. She carried one small bag. Zechariah stuck his head out the doorway, no doubt looking for Mary's parents. But there was no one in sight, save Mary.

"I greet you in the name of our most gracious Lord," Mary said, "who has given us promises sent by angels and children sent by God."

At Mary's greeting, I felt my baby leap inside. Filled with God's presence, I knew in that instant that Mary was Isaiah's virgin, the one who would bear God's Son.

A deep awe overcame me until words poured from my soul. "Mary, God has blessed you above all women, and your child is blessed!" Even the baby within my womb recognized the Messiah Mary carries.

Mary of Nazareth has the mature humility of a woman and the joy and wonder of a child. Oh, that God has chosen her for such a great task!

PONDERING . . .

1. What is your personal definition of envy? How does envy differ from jealousy? Where do you think these feelings come from?

2. If Elizabeth had allowed herself to be envious, list three things she could have envied about Mary. Imagine the consequences and loss, had there been envy between the two women. How have the consequences of envy affected your own life?

3. Romans 12:15 tells us to rejoice with those who rejoice, and to weep with those who weep. Is it harder for you to weep with those who weep, or to be happy with those who are happy? When have you missed out on sharing joy because you thought, *Why not me?*

4. How do you handle envy when it rears its ugly head? God is love, and he loves you as if you were the only one in the world. How does knowing how much God loves you help you get past feelings of envy or jealousy?

Dear God,
Great is your faithfulness—
always and in all ways.

MARY

DECEMBER 19

Understanding

And Mary said,
"My soul magnifies the Lord,
    and my spirit rejoices in God my Savior,
for he has looked with favor on the lowliness of his servant.
    Surely, from now on all generations will call me blessed;
for the Mighty One has done great things for me,
    and holy is his name.
His mercy is for those who fear him
    from generation to generation.
He has shown strength with his arm;
    he has scattered the proud in the thoughts of their hearts.
He has brought down the powerful from their thrones,
    and lifted up the lowly;
he has filled the hungry with good things,
    and sent the rich away empty.
He has helped his servant Israel,
    in remembrance of his mercy,
according to the promise he made to our ancestors,
    to Abraham and to his descendants forever."
                    (Luke 1:46–55)

●

Understanding

Elizabeth's understanding, that I carry the Son of God in my womb, lifted me above the weight of earth to the realm of heaven. When she said, "You are the most blessed of all women, and blessed is the child you will bear!" suddenly, my own praise burst from me like flood waters from the Jordan. I thanked Elohim for his faithfulness through all generations. Holy Scripture poured from my heart, memorized from the myriad of times my mother repeated the Scriptures to me as we milled barley to make bread, shaped flat bread, filled the oil lamps, or swept the floors.

When Zechariah failed to say one word to me, I feared his disapproval. But Elizabeth explained that when her husband had received the prophecy concerning his son and mine, a promise given to him by the angel Gabriel, Zechariah failed to believe. It is then that the angel left him without speech.

• • •

Over the next weeks, Zechariah and Elizabeth help to increase my understanding. They communicate with a tablet and with their eyes. Their son will prepare the world for what my son, the Messiah, must do. John—still an odd name to my ears—will preach repentance and forgiveness so that people may be ready for the salvation Jesus has come to offer.

Zechariah spends many hours opening the Scriptures to passages—about us.

About *us*.

Every day he begins with Isaiah: *Therefore the Lord himself will give you a sign: The virgin will conceive and give birth to a son, and will call him Immanuel* (Isaiah 7:14, NIV).

Today Zechariah had Elizabeth read, from the prophet Samuel, God's prophecy to David: *Your house and your kingdom shall be made sure forever before me; your throne shall be established forever* (2 Samuel 7:16).

It is just as the angel said.

PONDERING . . .

1. Think about where you are in life right now. Do you understand all parts of your current life?

2. Did any of your advance planning and carefully thought-out ideas fail to come through for you in the last year? What has been your reaction? How have you come to a better understanding of what really matters?

3. In what ways have God's plans been different from your own wishes for this season of life? What would you change if you had your way? Thank God for being in control, even if you just don't understand.

4. What adjustments can you make in your life that will help you focus on the birth and life of Jesus this Christmas? What can you do to keep your focus on Jesus after Christmas and throughout the new year?

Dear God,
Thank you for sharing your plan of
salvation with us through Scripture.

MARY

DECEMBER 20

Seek God's Kingdom

But seek first the kingdom of God
and His righteousness, and all these things
shall be added to you.
(Matthew 6:33, NKJV)

•

The LORD looks down from heaven on humankind
to see if there are any who are wise, who seek after God.
(Psalm 14:2)

•

One thing I have asked from the LORD,
that I shall seek:
That I may dwell in the house of
the LORD all the days of my life,
To behold the beauty of the LORD
And to meditate in His temple.
(Psalm 27:4, NASB)

•

"Come," my heart says, "seek his face!"
Your face, LORD, do I seek.
(Psalm 27:8)

•

Seek God's Kingdom

Lately, I find myself seeking God every morning, and he is always near. I join with the psalmist in answering the Lord's invitation to seek his face. My heart cries out, "Your face, O Lord, I shall seek." I believe I am in the center of God's will for me, as are Elizabeth and Zechariah.

Yet sometimes I ask myself, *Why isn't Elizabeth the chosen mother of our Savior?*

Why is Elizabeth and Zechariah's son to be the messenger to prepare the world for *my* son? Why has God chosen me to be the mother of his only Son? Elizabeth is blameless before God and wise beyond measure. She will make a wonderful mother, for she has proven to be a mother to me in my most needful hour. Her child will have a priest for a father, one who has entered the Holy Place. I don't even know if Joseph will follow through and wed me when he learns I am with child.

Yesterday Elizabeth and I sat beneath a tall cedar tree and gazed at the hills toward Jerusalem. Stillness and peace enveloped us while we listened to the mourning doves sing from a distant branch. The woodsy scent of the cedar calmed every anxious thought.

Suddenly, Elizabeth burst into laughter.

"What is it?" I asked.

She could not answer, but leaned back on our blanket and stroked her belly. "Mary, look at us—one old, dried-up Hebrew woman, and one child. Yet inside of us," she said, suddenly breathless, as with a sacred awe, "is the fate of the whole world."

She is great with child; my small body is still a child's. And the fate of all humanity is right here, on a worn blanket at the edge of a hill.

Such a plan! Our God in heaven must have as much humor as humility.

Elizabeth struggles to rise, "like a camel who has fallen asleep in a sandstorm," she says. How I would love to stay longer with Elizabeth and Zechariah, but this is Elizabeth's moment.

As for me, I must face Mother and Father and Joseph. I do not know what awaits me in Nazareth. But I do know that with me goes Immanuel.

PONDERING . . .

1. What do you think it means to seek God's kingdom? What would it mean for you to find God today? How will you look for him, and where will you look?

2. Matthew encourages his readers to seek first God's kingdom and his righteousness. If you made a list of priorities and put God first, what would numbers 2, 3, and 4 be? How do your actions and time reflect your priorities?

3. How do you seek God's kingdom?

4. God asks you to seek him with all your heart and all your soul. What have you been seeking as you get ready for Christmas? In these last days before Christmas, how can you help others find God's kingdom?

Dear God,
Help me seek your path and your kingdom
today and every day.

MARY

DECEMBER 21

Disappointment

Mary stayed with Elizabeth for about three months
and then returned home.

(Luke 1:56, NIV)

•

Now the birth of Jesus the Messiah took place in
this way. When his mother Mary had been engaged
to Joseph, but before they lived together, she
was found to be with child from the Holy Spirit.
Her husband Joseph, being a righteous man and
unwilling to expose her to public disgrace, planned
to dismiss her quietly.

(Matthew 1:18–19)

•

Because the Sovereign Lord helps me, I will not
be disgraced. Therefore, I have set my face like a
stone, determined to do his will. And I know that I
will not be put to shame.

(Isaiah 50:7, NLT)

●

And hope does not disappoint us, because God's love
has been poured into our hearts through the Holy
Spirit that has been given to us.

(Romans 5:5)

●

Disappointment

Poor Joseph.

Joseph of Nazareth is an excellent man, kind and forgiving. But he will not be my husband, and there will be no wedding ceremony. Joseph's sorrow weighs more heavily on him than his cloak of shame.

It seems the entire village knows I am with child. I believe there are as many rumors as villagers. Women in my supposed situation have been stoned, rocks cast from hands that once offered friendship and aid. Such punishment continues to this day.

Joseph has chosen to send me away quietly and without a public divorce, which would have ruined my mother's life in Nazareth.

I love my Joseph all the more for his generous decision. He is not vindictive or cruel. I had not expected cruelty to come from the kind Joseph I know. Yet I did believe he would choose a public divorce, and the accompanying shame of public humiliation.

Instead, dear Joseph will pay his own wages to send me away.

O *Lord, would not this kind and loving man have made the perfect husband for your maidservant? Would he not have been of inestimable value in raising up a son to your glory?*

PONDERING . . .

1. Have you ever been accused, or suspected, of something you didn't do? Have you known that you were a subject of gossip? Describe that feeling of being unjustly treated, or not believed.

2. Christmas can stir up disappointments within the family. When tensions begin to spoil Christmas, what might you do, or say, or pray to head off problems?

3. Jesus was born into a world that would reject him, accuse him of crimes he didn't commit, and ultimately crucify him. He would have to face the worst injustice in all of history, and his mother would have to watch. As you celebrate Christ's birth, how can you thoughtfully include Christ's death and resurrection into this Christmas season?

4. Are you ever disappointed in yourself? Ponder these five things God says about you: You are seen. You are heard. You are known. You are forgiven. You are loved.

*Dear God,
I have been disappointed. Thank you for
caring about me and my heartaches.*

MARY

DECEMBER 22

Compassion

But just when he had resolved to do this, an angel of the Lord appeared to him in a dream and said, "Joseph, son of David, do not be afraid to take Mary as your wife, for the child conceived in her is from the Holy Spirit. She will bear a son, and you are to name him Jesus, for he will save his people from their sins." All this took place to fulfill what had been spoken by the Lord through the prophet:

> "Look, the virgin shall conceive and bear a son,
>   and they shall name him Emmanuel,
>   which means, 'God is with us.'"

When Joseph awoke from sleep, he did as the angel of the Lord commanded him; he took her as his wife, but had no marital relations with her until she had borne a son; and he named him Jesus.

(Matthew 1:20–25)

●

Yet this I call to mind
and therefore I have hope:
Because of the Lord's great love
we are not consumed,
for his compassions never fail.
They are new every morning;
great is your faithfulness.
(Lamentations 3:21–23, NIV)

•

Compassion

O what a great and compassionate God we have! No one is like Elohim, who gives life, and remains faithful to the humblest of his servants.

As dawn was breaking, I stepped outside to gather sticks for the fire. There stood Joseph—*my* Joseph, his smile brighter than the sunrise. I could see myself fully adored in his eyes. My hair lay tangled at my shoulders, but never have I felt more beautiful, and never more loved.

Joseph fell to his knees before me. "Mary, I know. I *know*. I had a dream. I have been visited by an angel, who told me—!" He was too overcome with emotion to finish his words.

Peace flowed through me, and gratitude to Jehovah Shalom, the God of Peace, who has given insight and understanding to my Joseph. If Joseph and I can love each other with such faith and intensity, how much more must our Father in heaven love us!

• • •

We are wed. Joseph and I are man and wife! True, my wedding day was not as I had planned or dreamt about since I was old enough to dream. But Joseph and

I rejoice in God's faithful provision for our family and our future.

From the small window that opens to the courtyard, I often watch my husband. Houses here are close together and much alike, built on limestone blocks, some with flat roofs. Joseph has lived his entire life here. He shows his wares to the Roman soldiers, who have an unending need for yokes and wheels, tables and troughs. They pay in silver denarii, which Joseph's father sorely needs. Most of our neighbors pay in olive oil, wool, corn, or wood.

Joseph is a marvel. He works hard all day and well into the night, then returns and searches for ways he can care for me. We make plans, but I am struck by the littleness of every task, held next to the unimaginable responsibility given to us by Yahweh.

"Why did our great Jehovah choose me to raise his Son?" Joseph asks one night. "I used to wonder why the beautiful Mary should consent to be my bride. And now that I know the Son of God is to be my child, how much more do I ask myself, 'Why me?'!"

"God has wisely chosen you, Joseph of Nazareth," I reply. As the full moon spreads shadows across the courtyard, we sit together, filled with wonder.

PONDERING . . .

1. Why do you think God waited so long to reveal the truth and his plan to Joseph?

2. Try to imagine what Joseph might have been feeling at this point, wondering why God would have picked him. How often do you focus on God's plan for your life? Knowing God provides all you need to accomplish his will, how does this impact the way you live each day?

3. Count at least ten blessings God has given you. Filled with gratitude for God's grace, ask the Lord, "Why me?" How can you base your confidence on God?

4. What could you do differently this year to invite God to handle your expectations of Christmas Day and beyond?

Dear God,
Thank you for being compassionate and
loving toward me and my family.

MARY

DECEMBER 23

Flexibility

In those days a decree went out from Emperor
Augustus that all the world should be registered.
This was the first registration and was taken while
Quirinius was governor of Syria. All went to their
own towns to be registered. Joseph also went from
the town of Nazareth in Galilee to Judea, to the
city of David called Bethlehem, because he was
descended from the house and family of David. He
went to be registered with Mary, to whom he was
engaged and who was expecting a child.

(Luke 2:1–5)

•

But you, O Bethlehem of Ephrathah,
who are one of the little clans of Judah,
from you shall come forth for me
one who is to rule in Israel, whose origin is from of old,
from ancient days.

(Micah 5:2)

•

Flexibility

This morning I woke with the thought: Who will my son resemble? Will he look like all the other children? Will he be a helpless infant in every way? Will he hear the sounds of heaven?

He spoke and the worlds were made. Will he speak at birth?

When Joseph returned home, I wanted to ask for his thoughts, but he had news. "Caesar Augustus is demanding a worldwide census. Governor Quirinius agrees all Jews must be counted, no doubt for a tax!"

I remembered my father's complaint that the Romans take food from Jewish mouths and spend it on games. "Surely not another tax, Joseph?"

"There's more," he said. "Each family must go to its ancestral town. Since I descend from the house of Judah, I must travel to Bethlehem, the city of David."

I, too, descend from the line of David. My time grows near, and my strength decreases as the child in my womb increases. Yet I discern this census is somehow the will of God, and I must always bend to it. "We shall both go to Bethlehem."

In the middle of the night, I woke with laughter.

Joseph, startled, asked, "Mary, are you dreaming? Is it the baby?"

I shake my head. "Elizabeth and Zechariah showed me Micah's prophesy that the Messiah must be born in Bethlehem, though we could not imagine what would take me there."

I know the hand of the Almighty is wrapping us in his will, his ancient plan. I am gently folded into prophecy and becoming part of its fulfillment so it may bloom for the glory of the Ancient of Days and the Giver of Life. Amen.

• • •

We are on our journey. By day, we skirt the hills of Samaria, keeping our distance, crossing the valley east to the Jordan River, down the Jordan valley into the high Judean plateau, where a dusting of snow whitens the landscape. We have seen so many Roman soldiers, men like the officers in Nazareth, yet angrier. More threatening. They race their steeds, and we must scurry to get out of their way.

I slow down our journey to such an extent that I fear I shall be forced to give birth on the road.

PONDERING . . .

1. Where do your travels take you this Christmas? Across the room? Across town? Across the country? Are you confident that wherever you are, you're in the center of God's will for your life?

2. Mary's world changed dramatically, and she responded with trust and flexibility. How flexible are you? How do you handle change?

3. Think of three big changes you've had to deal with in the past year. How did you react during those times? Romans 8:28 promises that God will make all things work together for good for those who love him and are called according to his purpose. Looking back, can you see anything good that has come out of circumstances you considered undesirable at the time?

4. Have your Christmas Day celebrations changed over the years? What do you miss? What changes are you glad to have made?

Dear God,
Thank you for being alongside me on this
journey, wherever it may lead.

MARY

DECEMBER 24

Mysteries

Joseph therefore went from the town of Nazareth in Galilee to Judea, to the city of David called Bethlehem, because he was of the house and family of David. He went to be registered together with Mary, his betrothed, who was expecting a child. While they were there, the time came for her to have her child, and she gave birth to her firstborn son. She wrapped him in swaddling clothes and laid him in a manger, because there was no room for them in the inn.

(Luke 2:4–7, NCB)

•

Truly, O God of Israel, our Savior, you work in
mysterious ways.
(Isaiah 45:15, NLT)

●

. . . *that is*, the mystery which had been hidden from
the *past* ages and generations, but now has been
revealed to His saints, to whom God willed to make
known what the wealth of the glory of this mystery
among the Gentiles is, *the mystery* that is Christ in
you, the hope of glory.
(Colossians 1:26–27, NASB)

●

Mysteries

After days of journey, we are in Bethlehem, not far from Jerusalem. Snow-covered pilgrims flow into the village, tie their beasts, and sleep where they stop—in doorways, in the street. Tonight the small village is alive with foreign tongues. Surely the Tower of Babel could not have had more! Joseph asked for lodging at an inn, but they are filled.

Wrapped in my cloak, I rest by the gate with our belongings, while Joseph searches for a room. The smells of spiced meats, winter furs, and unpleasant travel odors add to my nausea.

It grows dark and cold, and beautiful snowflakes gather in mounds. Joseph still has not returned. God has told us this birth will take place in Bethlehem—and my womb agrees. Certainly, my husband will find a worthy place for the birth of the Savior.

From across the square, lights from olive oil lanterns glow warm as those inside houses prepare for the night. I am not the only woman with child in Bethlehem. *What will other children think of mine?* I wonder.

Ooh! Such a strong push from the life within me! *Joseph, where are you?*

At last, Joseph returns. "Mary, everywhere I seek lodging, others have already been turned away. I have gained no entrance into any Jewish home."

His desperate eyes stir my heart. I rise, straighten the folds of my tunic, adjust my veil and head covering. "Perhaps they will have more trouble turning down a mother with child."

Joseph protests, but seeing my determination, leads the way to the inn.

"If you were Quirinius himself, I could not find you a room!" The innkeeper shakes his head, then appears to look down and notice my belly. All he says is, "When?"

"Now," I answer. I feel God's life pressing to get out to the world.

The innkeeper falls silent. Then he says, "There is the stable."

Joseph's eyes reflect the consternation of his heart. "A stable?"

"You are welcome to bed there until you find better." He shrugs and turns to go.

Joseph starts after him, but I touch his shoulder. He stops and turns to me. "Mary, a stable? For the long-awaited Messiah?"

"Was it not Isaiah the prophet who said, 'Truly, O God of Israel, our Savior, you work in mysterious ways'? Perhaps our son will wait until tomorrow, and we can move into the inn. Tonight I welcome a bed of straw."

Joseph wraps his strong arm around me, and I lean entirely on him as we make our way past wine-happy travelers to the stable, cut into the rock behind the inn. God's creatures fill the barn—donkeys, horses, a goat, even a camel tied outside.

The pangs of childbirth commence. Joseph runs from the stable in search of a midwife. I cry out in pain and wish for my mother, or dear Elizabeth. I find my heart in a struggle. For nine months, the child has rested in me and me alone. A singular blessing.

This will no longer be true. I must share the Son of God with the world.

Oh that every woman could have the Son of God inside her for all her life!

PONDERING . . .

1. In the Apostle Paul's letter to the Colossians, he refers to the mystery that is now revealed, the mystery which is Christ in you, the hope of glory (Colossians1:27). Is Christ in you? How do you know?

2. Where were you born? Why do you think God chose to have his Son born in a stable?

3. Think about God's "mysterious ways" in the lives of Mary and Joseph. And think about God's mysterious ways in your own life.

4. What "mysteries" would you like to know about your future? Why do you think God doesn't reveal everything—past, present, future—to us right now?

Dear God,
Praise to you for the mystery of Jesus'
birth—our Savior, Messiah,
Redeemer, and King.

MARY

DECEMBER 25

Miracle

Merry Christmas!

For to us a child is born,
to us a son is given,
and the government will be on his shoulders.
And he will be called
Wonderful Counselor, Mighty God,
Everlasting Father, Prince of Peace.
Of the greatness of his government and peace
there will be no end.
He will reign on David's throne
and over his kingdom,
establishing and upholding it
with justice and righteousness
from that time on and forever.
The zeal of the Lord Almighty
will accomplish this.
(Isaiah 9:6–7, NIV)

•

So it was, that while they were there, the days were completed for her to be delivered. And she brought forth her firstborn Son, and wrapped Him in swaddling cloths, and laid Him in a manger, because there was no room for them in the inn.

(Luke 2:6–7, NKJV)

•

Now there were in the same country shepherds living out in the fields, keeping watch over their flock by night. And behold, an angel of the Lord stood before them, and the glory of the Lord shone around them, and they were greatly afraid. Then the angel said to them, "Do not be afraid, for behold, I bring you good tidings of great joy which will be to all people. For there is born to you this day in the city of David a Savior, who is Christ the Lord. And this *will be* the sign to you: You will find a Babe wrapped in swaddling cloths, lying in a manger."

And suddenly there was with the angel a multitude of the heavenly host praising God and saying:

"Glory to God in the highest,
And on earth peace, goodwill toward men!"

(Luke 2:8–14, NKJV)

•

So it was, when the angels had gone away from them into heaven, that the shepherds said to one another, "Let us now go to Bethlehem and see this thing that has come to pass, which the Lord has made known to us." And they came with haste and found Mary and Joseph, and the Babe lying in a manger. Now when they had seen *Him*, they made widely known the saying which was told them concerning this Child. And all those who heard *it* marveled at those things which were told them by the shepherds. But Mary kept all these things and pondered *them* in her heart. Then the shepherds returned, glorifying and praising God for all the things that they had heard and seen, as it was told them.

(Luke 2:15–20, NKJV)

•

Miracle

After hours of pain, I have delivered the perfect child. It is enough of my Lord's miracle to experience a birth, to see life come from my body. But that this tiny baby, lying in a manger, is God's own Son—it is more than I can hold in my mind.

Joseph is so tender, though he hardly knows what to do. We work as one. Joseph made a bed of straw in a narrow trough. I wrapped our child in strips of cloth as I have seen many others do. The trough is rough stone, but Jesus does not seem to mind.

I had drifted off to sleep when Joseph, suddenly alert, cried, "Who's there?"

A small boy stepped out of the shadows. Behind him came other men in robes with staffs. Their hair hung long, their faces furrowed leather, concealing their age. They smelled of the sheep they undoubtedly guard.

I watched in silence as they knelt at the manger and praised God. Joseph and I exchanged looks of astonishment. How could these poor shepherds know?

One of the shepherds began talking. His dialect proved hard to understand—more difficult as he talked faster, carried along by his own words of angels and choirs from heaven. "An angel burst through the sky! Knew how scared we were and said, 'Do not be afraid! I have good news of great joy for all people.' And that includes us shepherds. Then the angel said that right now, right here, a Savior was born, who is Christ the Lord. And he gave us a sign that we'd find that baby wrapped in swaddling clothes in a manger!"

There was more—a bright star, armies of angels. "And so," the shepherd concluded, "we have come to worship the newborn king."

Wonder of wonders! I believe the words of angels and prophets. This child is the Savior, the long-awaited Messiah, God's Only Son, God with Us.

And yet, he is my son as well, my baby. I pray that God will give me grace that I might be the mother God intends, neither holding too tightly nor too feebly.

God has sent us Jesus, who has entered our world so that we may enter his and have life everlasting.

These things I will treasure. These truths I will ponder in my heart.

PONDERING . . .

1. Luke tells us that Mary treasured everything that happened, all that was said, on that first Christmas. What are your earliest Christmas memories? What will you remember from today?

2. How many Christmas gifts from past years can you recall? Is there something about those gifts that makes them worth remembering? Thank God the Father for the Gift of Jesus Christ and consider why he is worth remembering and thanking.

3. Imagine the conflicts Mary must have experienced. God's Son, Ruler, King, Messiah, Prince of Peace, Wonderful Counselor, Immanuel, God with Us, was still her infant. How would she handle fully human Baby Jesus? Toddler Jesus? Teen Jesus? Jesus in his ministry?

4. How would your life be different if Jesus had not been born?

Dear God,
Thank you for sending your beloved Son,
Jesus, to die for our sins.

ELIZABETH

DECEMBER 26

Obedience

When it was time for Elizabeth to have her baby, she gave birth to a son. Her neighbors and relatives heard that the Lord had shown her great mercy, and they shared her joy.

(Luke 1:57–58, NIV)

•

On the eighth day they came to circumcise the child, and they were going to name him after his father Zechariah, but his mother spoke up and said, "No! He is to be called John."

(Luke 1:59–60, NIV)

•

And this is love: that we walk in obedience to his
commands. As you have heard from the beginning,
his command is that you walk in love.

(2 John 1:6, NIV)

•

I was silent and still;
I held my peace to no avail;
my distress grew worse,
my heart became hot within me.
While I mused, the fire burned;
then I spoke with my tongue.

(Psalm 39:2–3)

•

Obedience

What a wonder is our God, who creates us from dust and continues the miracle of procreation in his image! Already, John's spontaneous cries sound to me as if our little prophet is crying out his yet unintelligible message.

Today our son, the chosen Elijah, turned eight days old. This is an important day prescribed in our Law, the Day of Circumcision, the Naming Day. I admit that my old body was weary at dawn, but Zechariah and I were eager for our child to enter into the sign of the covenant our God has made with us. For me, the ceremony was to be a public promise that we would raise our son according to God's law.

Friends and relatives greeted us warmly. So many share in our miraculous joy, this child born from our ancient bodies. How I wish Mary and Joseph could be with us! I pray our gracious Lord blesses their holy family.

When the rabbi arrived for the circumcision ceremony, my husband welcomed him wordlessly. All present knew the Lord had taken away Zechariah's speech in the Holy Place when he'd failed to believe the angel. Speech did not return to my husband at our son's birth.

The rabbi showed no signs of offense at Zechariah's silence as the ceremony commenced. It was in the middle of the ceremony when the rabbi put his hand on our child's head and said, "And you, small Zechariah, will follow in your father's—"

But I heard no more. *Zechariah?* Panic rose within me. The rabbi had not spoken with me before the ceremony, of course. Since my husband could not speak himself, the rabbi assumed we were giving our son his father's name, as is the custom.

Yet God had clearly named our son "John." How could I allow the sacred naming to go against God's will and command? I had never spoken in a service or a ceremony, but something had to be done.

I looked to my husband and pleaded with my eyes for him to do something. Poor Zechariah looked as distressed as I. Yet he could not speak.

It was up to me. "No!" I shouted, surprising myself as much as the rabbi. "His name is John."

PONDERING . . .

1. Have you ever had to stand up to someone in authority in order to obey what you knew God wanted you to do?

2. How can we know we're insisting, or arguing, for God's will or for our own?

3. What does your name mean? Does your name hold special significance in your family's genealogy? The angel Gabriel named John and Jesus. Why were their names so important?

4. Elizabeth was obedient to God's command to name her child "John." What do you think the word "obedient" means? How do you feel when you're told to be "obedient"?

Dear God,
Help me obey your direction,
and give me confidence to follow your
commandments.

ELIZABETH

DECEMBER 27

Tender Mercies

But his mother said, "No; he is to be called John." They said to her, "None of your relatives has this name." Then they began motioning to his father to find out what name he wanted to give him. He asked for a writing tablet and wrote, "His name is John." And all of them were amazed. Immediately his mouth was opened and his tongue freed, and he began to speak, praising God. Fear came over all their neighbors, and all these things were talked about throughout the entire hill country of Judea. All who heard them pondered them and said, "What then will this child become?" For, indeed, the hand of the Lord was with him.

(Luke 1:60–66)

•

Then his father Zechariah was filled with the Holy Spirit and profesied:

(Luke 1:67)

•

"And you, my child, will be called a prophet of
   the Most High;
for you will go on before the Lord to prepare the
   way for him,
to give his people the knowledge of salvation
through the forgiveness of their sins,
because of the tender mercy of our God,
by which the rising sun will come to us from heaven
to shine on those living in darkness
and in the shadow of death, to guide our feet into
   the path of peace."

(Luke 1:76–79, NIV)

•

Tender Mercies

The rabbi and our relatives looked on in horror at my pronouncement that our son's name is John. Not only had I, a woman, spoken in such a solemn ceremony, but no one in the family had such a name.

All turned to Zechariah, who—far from looking astonished—appeared more relieved than I have seen him for quite some time. Though he nodded with ferocious intent his agreement with me, he uttered not a word.

Suddenly, his hands flew in the air, reminding me of the day my mute husband returned from the temple with Gabriel's message. As I understood then, I understood once again. Zechariah was motioning for a tablet.

We all watched in silence as he took the offered tablet and began writing with strong, but shaky hands: *His name is John.*

At the moment of Zechariah's obedient proclamation, in the stillness of the room, with friends and relatives straining to see, Zechariah's tongue was loosened. What began as groans from a closed throat, soon became the music of praise. Reverence seized us as my husband praised our God, who has come to redeem his people as he promised long ages past, our God of tender mercies!

Tears welled up from the depth of my heart, and I joined my husband's praise. Our great God has such tender mercies, and he has remembered us this day, a day spoken of by prophets.

Our child, John, will be called a prophet of the Most High. Zechariah announced to the whole assembly that John will prepare the way for the Messiah. Our son must preach repentance and God's salvation, for all must turn from disobedience and sin, and turn to the Savior.

What an honor! And what a responsibility for such a tiny, miraculous baby!

PONDERING . . .

1. What character traits do you see in Elizabeth that you would like to build in your own life? How can you take steps to develop those qualities?

2. John the Baptist's mission was to deliver God's message: "Repent, for the kingdom of heaven is at hand." What do you think "repent" means? How would repenting "prepare the way" for salvation in Christ? How would you explain to a friend the need to repent?

3. Psalm 51 is about sin, repentance, and forgiveness. The first verse says: *Have mercy upon me, O God, According to Your lovingkindness; According to the multitude of Your tender mercies, Blot out my transgressions* (Psalm 51:1, NKJV). What significance do the words "lovingkindness" and "tender mercies" have for you? How do they relate to forgiveness, or blotting out your transgressions?

4. What tender mercies have you received or witnessed?

Dear God,
Thank you for providing tender mercies
with each new day.

ANNA

DECEMBER 28

Rituals

When Aaron has finished making atonement for the Most Holy Place, the tent of meeting and the altar, he shall bring forward the live goat. He is to lay both hands on the head of the live goat and confess over it all the wickedness and rebellion of the Israelites—all their sins—and put them on the goat's head. He shall send the goat away into the wilderness in the care of someone appointed for the task. The goat will carry on itself all their sins to a remote place; and the man shall release it in the wilderness.

(Leviticus 16:20–22, NIV)

•

"I bring no charges against you concerning your sacrifices or concerning your burnt offerings, which are ever before me. I have no need of a bull from your stall or of goats from your pens, for every animal of the forest is mine, and the cattle on a thousand hills."

(Psalm 50:8–10, NIV)

•

For by grace you have been saved through faith;
and this is not of yourselves, it is the gift of God;
not a result of works, so that no one may boast.
(Ephesians 2:8–9, NASB)

●

And Abram believed the LORD, and the LORD counted
him as righteous because of his faith.
(Genesis 15:6, NLT)

●

Rituals

During my lifetime of service in the temple, I have considered our religious rituals, and I have come to understand that the Almighty requires rituals, not as tests or works to grant us salvation, but as messages to lead us into a relationship with him. In themselves, rituals earn us nothing, but they can lead us into grace. Only God can gift us with salvation, or righteousness. Abraham himself was deemed righteous because of his faith in God, not because of his obedience to the Law or his good works.

I love and value the Jewish rituals, which paint a picture of God's truth. Yesterday, I spoke with a young woman who, too poor to purchase a lamb, brought two pigeons for sacrifice. "God wants our hearts of devotion more than our livestock," I told her.

Each year, I wait eagerly for the Day of Atonement, when the High Priest first sacrifices a bull for his own sin, then selects two goats and sacrifices one. He lays his hands on the live goat's head, the "scapegoat," and confesses the sins of the people, placing our sins onto the goat, which will carry them into the wilderness. This ritual is a beautiful picture of God's gracious plan for our salvation. He will sacrifice the Messiah by placing our sins upon him and granting us forgiveness.

At times, I watch the temple priests, the Sadducees, who dominate the temple proceedings and tend to align with Rome. In the streets, I observe Pharisees, who gain their power in synagogues. Always in their blue-fringed cloaks, they perform their duties publicly, offering favors to the wealthy. I pray they do not rely on their own righteousness.

I, too, perform my duties, worshiping, praying, fasting, telling others of God's plan of redemption. I do not consider these actions "duties," because they come from my heart and bring me such joy.

There is a saying that the only truly free person is a widow. Perhaps there is truth in the adage. Though I spend my days and nights serving in the temple, I experience the Lord's freedom each day.

PONDERING . . .

1. What are your thoughts surrounding church rituals, such as communion, baptism, weddings, and funerals? What do you think each ritual or tradition represents?

2 What do spiritual rituals mean to you? Are there any rituals you observed early in life that you miss having as part of your current worship experience?

3. Do you have any "rituals" of your own? How can you adopt spiritual practices into your daily life and make each routine more meaningful, or personal?

4. Paul writes: *For it is by grace you have been saved, through faith—and this is not from yourselves, it is the gift of God—not by works, so that no one can boast* (Ephesians 2:8–9, NIV). What does it mean for you to be "saved by grace"? What would it mean to be saved by works? What would it mean for salvation to be a combination of grace and works?

Dear God,
Thank you for the gift of grace. May I show grace to those I meet today.

ANNA

DECEMBER 29

Endurance

He gives power to the faint, and strengthens the
powerless. Even youths will faint and be weary,
and the young will fall exhausted;
but those who wait for the LORD shall renew their
strength, they shall mount up with wings like
eagles, they shall run and not be weary, they shall
walk and not faint.
(Isaiah 40:29–31)

•

Do not fear, for I am with you,
do not be afraid, for I am your God;
I will strengthen you, I will help you,
I will uphold you with my victorious right hand.
(Isaiah 41:10)

•

The Lord your God in your midst,
The Mighty One, will save;
He will rejoice over you with gladness, He will
quiet *you* with His love,
He will rejoice over you with singing.
(Zephaniah 3:17, NKJV)

•

The righteous flourish like the palm tree, and
grow like a cedar in Lebanon.
They are planted in the house of the Lord; they
flourish in the courts of our God.
In old age they still produce fruit; they are always
green and full of sap.
(Psalm 92:12–14)

•

Endurance

Today I am feeling every one of my 84 years. As I walked the temple grounds, my legs fought to give way beneath me. Breath came in short, hard-earned draws that threatened to lodge in my throat. Once I was inside the Court of Women, the chill remained in my bones, preventing my fingers from bending in prayer. I chose to ignore my rebellious and shouting knees and knelt in my quiet corner. Many have found peace here in the women's court, overlooked by tall lampstands in each corner.

For older worshipers, it is tempting to convince ourselves that the best is behind us. "Remember the days when . . .?" we whisper, recalling only the brighter moments of youth. Yet in my spirit, I know the best is ahead of me. I am still here for a reason.

A young woman passes by and lifts her two children, one in each arm, with a strength that abandoned me long ago. I offer up a secret smile with Jehovah-Elohim, my Creator, who knows this earthen vessel he created. I must depend on his mighty strength, rather than my own. And this is a benefit of old age. Every ache serves as a reminder that God is my strength. This reliance gives me an intimacy with my Lord that I lacked during younger years.

I thank the Lord for the blessings of old age and pray that, as with Moses, God will teach me to number my days and give me a heart of wisdom.

When I look up, sunlight shines a path on my little corner, entering my bones as the glorious light of God enters my soul. Perhaps I have needed all this time so that I will recognize the Savior when he comes.

PONDERING . . .

1. In Anna's time, people sought advice from the elderly, who were well respected. How have times changed? What can you do to show respect for older people in your family and in your community?

2. Paul wrote to the believers in Corinth: *But we have this treasure in clay jars, so that it may be made clear that this extraordinary power belongs to God and does not come from us* (2 Corinthians 4:7). How do you handle aches and pains? How could you, like Anna, draw closer to God with every passing year?

3. When the Apostle Paul suffered from weakness in his eyes, Jesus encouraged him: *But he said to me, "My grace is sufficient for you, for power is made perfect in weakness." So, I will boast all the more gladly of my weaknesses, so that the power of Christ may dwell in me* (2 Corinthians 12:9). When have you experienced Christ's power in the face of your own weakness?

4. What comes to mind when you think about the "good ol' days"? What promises does God offer you for your future?

Dear God,
Renew my strength.
Bring healing to the sick. Transform us in
our weakness.

MARY

DECEMBER 30

Humility

If a woman conceives and bears a male child, she
shall be ceremonially unclean seven days; as at the
time of her menstruation, she shall be unclean.
On the eighth day the flesh of his foreskin shall be
circumcised. Her time of blood purification shall
be thirty-three days; she shall not touch any holy
thing, or come into the sanctuary, until the days
of her purification are completed.

(Leviticus 12:2–4)

·

He has told you, O mortal, what is good;
and what does the Lord require of you
but to do justice, and to love kindness,
and to walk humbly with your God?

(Micah 6:8)

·

Do nothing out of selfish ambition or vain conceit. Rather, in humility value others above yourselves, not looking to your own interests but each of you to the interests of the others. In your relationships with one another, have the same mindset as Christ Jesus: Who, being in very nature God, did not consider equality with God something to be used to his own advantage; rather, he made himself nothing by taking the very nature of a servant, being made in human likeness. And being found in appearance as a man, he humbled himself by becoming obedient to death—even death on a cross!

(Philippians 2:3–8, NIV)

•

Humility

Joseph and I must stay in Bethlehem, near enough to Jerusalem that we are able to observe all the ceremonies required by Jewish law. How strange it is that the Messiah and Son of God should be dedicated and consecrated, though he comes directly from the Father of all Creation. Such a covenant seems unnecessary for this child. Joseph says Jesus will set the godly example for all people, and obedience needs to be modeled in order for it to be followed. Immanuel will live as all humans live, be tempted in all things, but commit no sin.

On the eighth day after his birth, Jesus was circumcised and officially named, as the Law requires. It is also tradition for a firstborn son to be presented to God after birth. The ceremony involves a "redeeming," or a buying back of the child from God through an offering. For forty days after my son's birth, I was considered ceremonially unclean and could not enter the temple, of course.

Now we are at an end to my forty-day separation. Joseph and I have received no visits from the rabbis, or the royal court, though we might have cause to fear such a visit from Herod, known for his cruelty and jealousy. Jesus does not appear to be recognized as Immanuel, God with Us, nor as the Messiah, the Savior of the world.

When I consider there is no recognition other than from the shepherds, I am tempted to feel wronged. Then I ponder the humility of God's Son, who left the throne of heaven to be held inside my womb for nine months. Considering how God humbled himself, the least I can do is humble myself in thanksgiving and praise to the Giver of Life.

Joseph and I have been preparing for the short journey to Jerusalem, where we plan to fulfill the requirements for my purification and to consecrate our son. The Law requires we bring a lamb for a burnt offering and a turtledove for a sin offering. This, we fervently wish we could do. But we can barely afford the price of a pigeon. Fortunately, our loving Lord understands, for the Law adds that if we cannot afford a lamb, we are allowed to bring two doves or pigeons instead. This is what we must humbly do.

PONDERING . . .

1. How would you define "humility"? In what ways were Mary, Elizabeth, and Anna humble? Do you think you're humble? Why, or why not?

2. If Mary had lacked humility, how might she have acted after the angel Gabriel's announcement? Why do you think she kept her silence? What do you think kept Elizabeth from racing to tell everyone that she was pregnant?

3. One definition of humility is thinking rightly of yourself—not too high, not too low. In the few verses about Anna the Prophetess, what evidence of humility can you see? What are areas in your life that tempt you to think too highly, or too lowly, of yourself?

4. List ways that Jesus Christ chose to walk humbly throughout his life on earth.

Dear God,
Help me to do justice, and to love kindness,
and to walk humbly.

ANNA

DECEMBER 31

1

Fulfillment

Now there was a man in Jerusalem whose name was Simeon; this man was righteous and devout, looking forward to the consolation of Israel, and the Holy Spirit rested on him. It had been revealed to him by the Holy Spirit that he would not see death before he had seen the Lord's Messiah. Guided by the Spirit, Simeon came into the temple; and when the parents brought in the child Jesus, to do for him what was customary under the law, Simeon took him in his arms and praised God, saying,

"Master, now you are dismissing your servant in
    peace,
      according to your word;
      for my eyes have seen your salvation,
      which you have prepared in the presence of all
      peoples,
a light for revelation to the Gentiles
and for glory to your people Israel."

And the child's father and mother were amazed at what was being said about him. Then Simeon blessed them and said to his mother Mary, "This child is destined for the falling and the rising of many in Israel, and to be a sign that will be opposed so that the inner thoughts of many will be revealed—and a sword will pierce your own soul too."

(Luke 2:25–35)

●

Fulfillment

This day in the temple, where I had been in deep prayer and supplication, I heard Simeon's voice above all others. Such strength of voice is not a usual occurrence from this devout servant of God, whose age surpasses my own. Simeon comes often to the temple. We have talked together in the Court of Women, and I have always known that he is filled with the Spirit of God and waiting for the redemption of Israel.

A child had been brought to the temple for dedication. Short in stature, I could not see the babe until Simeon took the child and lifted him up, praising God: "Sovereign Lord, as you have promised, you may now dismiss your servant in peace. For my eyes have seen your salvation, which you have prepared in the sight of all nations: a light for revelation to the Gentiles, and the glory of your people Israel" (Luke 2:29–32, NIV).

Simeon's age-old eyes shone with overflowing joy, as did my own. At once, I recognized this was God's Messiah. The priests went about their business, seemingly unmoved by this miraculous appearance of the Promised One.

Simeon blessed the child's parents, then turned to the young mother. "This child is destined to cause the falling and rising of many in Israel, and to be a sign that will be spoken against, so that the thoughts of many hearts will be revealed. And a sword will pierce your own soul too" (Luke 2:34–35, NIV).

Such a hard prophecy, but I have read the same prophecies and know this child will suffer for our sins.

So amazed was I, so overcome with gratitude, I had hardly noticed the child's mother. Then I looked at her, and her adoration for the child lit her very being. Was there ever such an honor as to be the mother of God's Son and Messiah? Out of all the women God created, he chose this young girl standing so close to me I might have put my arm around her.

Simeon had just prophesied of the opposition waiting for her son, and he warned her that a sword would pierce her soul. I could see the message already weighing on the mother's small shoulders.

PONDERING . . .

1. Why do you think God chose Simeon to prophesy about Jesus? The Lord promised Simeon that he wouldn't die until he saw the Messiah. Are there people in your life that you hope will recognize the Messiah? Pray for their salvation and God's mighty love to wrap around them in miraculous ways.

2. What have you prayed for and had to wait years before God answered? If you received what you prayed for, were you surprised by his answer? Did God answer exactly the way you had hoped?

3. What do you think Simeon meant about a sword piercing Mary's heart? What things "pierce" your own heart? What kinds of things make your heart break?

4. Imagine what Mary and Joseph's expectations may have been as they fulfilled their duty as parents. What are your spiritual expectations for life in the New Year?

Dear God,
Shine your light on the nations and help me
be a light in the darkness.

ANNA

JANUARY 1

Prophesying

At that moment she [Anna] came, and began to
praise God and to speak about the child to all who
were looking for the redemption of Jerusalem.

(Luke 2:38)

•

Give praise to the LORD, proclaim his name;
make known among the nations what he has done.
Sing to him, sing praise to him;
tell of all his wonderful acts.

(1 Chronicles 16:8–9, NIV)

•

Prophesying

As I looked on with the temple crowd at the dedication of the Messiah, I could barely restrain my joy and gratitude. Before me was the fulfillment of God's promise to bring about redemption. All the prophecies from all ages are fulfilled in this child. Heaven and earth have met, and my soul shouts, "Hallelujah!"

God's purpose for me has been to prophesy toward this moment, for this Savior. Other prophetesses, named and unnamed, have gone before me: Sarah, wife of Abraham and mother of Isaac; Hannah, the good mother of Samson; Miriam, who is the first named prophetess in our history. There was Deborah, a prophetess and judge; the unnamed prophetess who became Isaiah's wife; Huldah, the prophetess King Josiah asked to interpret the Word of the Lord when the Book of the Law was found. And there were others. God chose them to "foretell" events to come, and to "forth-tell," carrying forward his message.

I was aware of the priests performing the purification rites and dedication, though they showed no sign of amazement, or even interest in Jesus. This puzzled me, but still my heart filled with praise for such a God, who sent the Savior in the form of a tiny human.

I longed to hold the Messiah as Simeon had done! But that is not why our Lord has kept me in his temple. Over the years of waiting, God has changed me. He has drawn me close. Early in my widowhood, would I have recognized the Messiah? Would I have had the boldness to speak about salvation through the Messiah?

I gave thanks to El Shaddai, God Almighty, the Mighty One of Jacob, for sending his Son. Then I turned to the worshipers and spoke about the Messiah to all who were looking forward to the redemption of Israel. They needed to understand that their Messiah has arrived. This tiny king is the Son of God, our Redeemer and Savior.

For the remainder of my days, I will live in the temple to tell all who will listen of the glory of God with Us, our Savior Messiah.

Surely your goodness and unfailing love will pursue
me all the days of my life,
and I will live in the house of the Lord forever.
(Psalm 23:6, NLT)

PONDERING . . .

1. How do you think Anna recognized Jesus the Messiah? In what ways might she have changed as she grew older in the temple? How are you changing as you grow in your faith?

2. How did Anna know which worshipers had been waiting for the Messiah? How has the Holy Spirit given you insight or led you to minister in a specific way?

3. How do you know when the Holy Spirit is leading? What has kept you from the Holy Spirit's prompting, or guidance?

4. How might you naturally turn to people around you and tell them about Jesus? Is it difficult for you to speak with others about Christ? Why do you think it is, or isn't?

Dear God,
I will praise and lift your name all my days,
thankful for your unfailing love.

MARY

JANUARY 2

Hesed

And the child's father and mother were amazed at what was being said about him. Then Simeon blessed them and said to his mother Mary, "This child is destined for the falling and the rising of many in Israel, and to be a sign that will be opposed so that the inner thoughts of many will be revealed—and a sword will pierce your own soul too."

(Luke 2:33–35)

•

Show us Your lovingkindness, O Lᴏʀᴅ,
And grant us Your salvation.
(Psalm 85:7, ɴᴀsʙ 1995)

•

For your unfailing love is higher than the heavens.
Your faithfulness reaches to the clouds.
(Psalm 108:4, ɴʟᴛ)

•

English Translations of *Hesed*
in 1 Chronicles 16:34
(Emphases from the author)

"Give thanks to the Lord, for *He is* good;
For His *faithfulness* is everlasting." (NASB)

O give thanks to the Lord, for *He is* good; For His
lovingkindness is everlasting. (NASB 1995)

Give thanks to the Lord, for he is good;
his *love* endures forever. (NIV)

O give thanks to the Lord, for he is good;
for his *steadfast love* endures forever. (NRSV)

Give thanks to the Lord, for he is good!
His *faithful love* endures forever. (NLT)

Oh, give thanks to the Lord, for *He is* good! For His
mercy endures forever. (NKJV)

Give thanks to *Adonai*; for he is good, for his *grace*
continues forever. (CJB)

Give testimony about the Eternal because He is
good; His *loyal love* lasts forever. (VOICE)

Hesed

Today was the day of my purification and the dedication of Jesus. My thoughts still swirl like snowflakes in a blizzard.

With our sleeping child, Joseph and I approached the temple, passing through the eastern gate, where triumphant warriors have entered. Joseph steadied me as I stared up at the tall and massive temple complex, stones and thick walls stretching until I could not see their end. This second temple, rebuilt after the destruction of Solomon's Temple, is still under reconstruction by King Herod, though I will never call it "Herod's Temple."

We crossed the noisy Court of the Gentiles, treading on stones of various colors, past men arguing over cattle, birds, and coins. Between the Gentiles and the Court of Women runs a wall, the *soreg,* separating Gentiles from the rest of the temple. Signs etched in giant stones threaten death to Gentiles who enter. I know the Lord's Messiah will be the Light of Revelation to the Nations, Jews and Gentiles alike. Gentiles will not be shut out. I admit I am not fond of the Roman soldiers I have met. But God is.

We entered the Court of Women through the "Beautiful Gate," made of ornamental Corinthian brass. There we heard prophecies about Jesus . . . and me.

Jesus was recognized as the Messiah by an elderly prophet and a kind prophetess. What joy I felt in their declarations! Though others passed us with no notice, my heart soared in union with these godly believers. Prophesies spoke of the salvation the Messiah will bring in glory, but also of the downfall he will be to others. The old prophet called Simeon blessed us, but followed with the prophecies that disturb my soul, the soul that will be pierced by a sword. I am sure the prophesied rejection and pain awaiting Jesus will be the sword that will pierce my soul. I would rather have the sword of Goliath pierce my body.

Even through these warnings, I felt Adonai's *hesed* throughout the dedication. *Hesed* is a word taught to me by a rabbi when I was much younger. He said this word appears in the Holy Scriptures more than 250 times. *Hesed* combines God's mercy, compassion, unfailing love, grace, faithfulness, and lovingkindness. I have relied on God and his *hesed* to this day. I will continue to trust in the lovingkindness of El Elyon, our sovereign, Almighty God. His *hesed* will cover us all.

PONDERING . . .

1. Take time to meditate on God's *hesed*. How has God shown you mercy? Steadfast love? Faithfulness? Grace? Unfailing love? Lovingkindness?

2. In the Bible, *hesed* usually refers to God's relationship with us. Which word for *hesed* best describes your relationship with God: grace, love, lovingkindness, kindness, mercy, loyalty, unfailing love, compassion?

3. How do you see God's *hesed* in your relationships with others?

4. *Hesed* is also used in connection with human relationships. What relationships with family and friends have characteristics of *hesed*? Be specific.

Dear God,
I trust you and your everlasting kindness.
Salvation comes through Christ alone.

ELIZABETH

JANUARY 3

Prepare the Way

The beginning of the gospel of Jesus Christ, the Son of God. As it is written in the Prophets:

"Behold, I send My messenger before Your face,
Who will prepare Your way before You."
"The voice of one crying in the wilderness:
'Prepare the way of the Lord;
Make His paths straight.'"
(Mark 1:1–3, NKJV)

•

This messenger was John the Baptist. He was in the wilderness and preached that people should be baptized to show that they had repented of their sins and turned to God to be forgiven. All of Judea, including all the people of Jerusalem, went out to see and hear John. And when they confessed their sins, he baptized them in the Jordan River. His clothes were woven from coarse camel hair, and he wore a leather belt around his waist. For food he ate locusts and wild honey.

John announced:

"Someone is coming soon who is greater than I am—so much greater that I'm not even worthy to stoop down like a slave and untie the straps of his sandals. I baptize you with water, but he will baptize you with the Holy Spirit!"

(Mark 1:4–8, NLT)

•

Prepare the Way

Our son grows as fast as the gazelle! He is now six months in age, and I can barely carry him. I have aged as well, for it seems to take all I have to care for this child. I would have it no other way. And I thank our gracious God for our John every minute of every day.

We keep the Nazarite vows and have never once cut his hair, which is a sign of John's separation for God's use. I am grateful for this regulation, as I would miss his thick, black curls.

Zechariah thinks constantly of a program to train up his son in the ways of the Lord. He feels the weight of responsibility to entrust the Holy Scriptures to John. My husband worries, with his weakness and vision declining, that he might not be able to complete his mission with our son.

When I take John into Bethany, or even Jerusalem, heads turn. I hear the whispers as we pass. Even they discern that John has been set apart. Do the Roman soldiers see the same? Does Herod? What would he do if he knew of John's mission?

Then I remember. It is the Almighty who brought my son into this world—announced by an angel, conceived through the loins of an old man, into the dried-up womb of this old woman.

Surely my God will watch over this messenger and help John fulfill his mission.

PONDERING . . .

1. Imagine how Elizabeth must have felt as John moved into the wilderness and ate locusts and wild honey. Have you ever had to balance what you wanted for someone with what they wanted for themselves? What was difficult about this process?

2. In one sentence, state John the Baptist's mission and ministry. Why was it important to get John's message out before Jesus began his public ministry? How do you feel about sharing Jesus' message of salvation?

3. What do you know about Jesus and John's relationship as adults? Consider Jesus' baptism (Matthew 3:13–17); John's imprisonment (Matthew 11:4–18); Jesus' reaction to John's death (Matthew 14:6–14).

4. John told people that he wasn't worthy to untie Jesus' sandals, something done by slaves. Jesus told his disciples that among those born on earth, no one was greater than John the Baptist. What qualities of Elizabeth do you see in her son? What qualities honor God?

Dear God,
Help me prepare the way for those who do
not have a relationship with Jesus Christ.

MARY

JANUARY 4

Seek His Face

The Lord looks down from heaven on the entire
human race; he looks to see if anyone is truly
wise, if anyone seeks God.

(Psalm 14:2, NLT)

•

My heart says of you, "Seek his face!"
Your face, Lord, I will seek.

(Psalm 27:8, NIV)

•

You hide them in the shelter of your presence, safe
from those who conspire against them. You shelter
them in your presence, far from accusing tongues.

(Psalm 31:20, NLT)

•

From there you will seek the Lord your God, and
you will find him if you search after him with all
your heart and soul.
(Jeremiah 29:13)

●

"Ask, and it will be given to you; seek, and you will
find; knock, and it will be opened to you."
(Matthew 7:7, NASB)

●

Seek His Face

Joseph left this morning to find work here in Bethlehem. Without his father's carpenter shop, Joseph must find work wherever he can, whenever he can.

It is evening when my husband returns with deep sighing. Darkness has crept in early, and the moon chooses to hide behind the clouds. He walks directly to me and lifts Jesus from my lap. Holding him up that they may be face to face, he says, "All day I sought labor, Mary. I asked to help at building projects of Herod—the city's fortification wall, digging on the aqueducts. If I heard chisel and stone, I chased the sound. But after a day of seeking work, I have come home with empty hands." He lowers Jesus into my arms and grins at me as if he cannot help himself. "I did find something. More rumors of Herod, the 'Great King of the Jews,' as his Roman masters call him."

For as long as I have lived, longer even than my parents have been on the earth, the Romans have ruled over us. Tyrannical Herod is no more than their puppet. "What is it this time, Joseph? More taxes? Another lavish feast for his Romans?"

"Yes, that." His face alters as he kneels beside me and touches our son's cheek. "People say Herod is more fearful than ever, believing he may be replaced. His soldier-bodyguards have increased to two thousand, and his spies are everywhere. I worry what he might do if he finds out that our son is the true King of Kings."

For an instant, my heart rises in defense of my son. How can I protect him? How can Joseph? A moment earlier, my thoughts were how to feed our child if Joseph cannot work. And now—!

But then my heart turns to Jehovah-Jireh, "The Lord Will Provide." And I am found by him. As I seek him above all else, I find peace in his loving arms. "Joseph, we will continue to seek God and his protection, and he will continue to provide."

At this, my husband smiles and takes our child that I may serve our meal: barley bread with a bit of olive oil. As Joseph offers our thanks to Elohim, inwardly, I ask for God's grace to seek him in every moment and live in the light of his presence.

PONDERING . . .

1. What do you think it means to "seek the Lord"? What can you do today to look for Jesus in your everyday routine?

2. What do you generally seek when you're worried? How can it help to "seek God's face" when problems surround us? How can we do this in practical ways?

3. In Matthew 6, right before Jesus says to seek him first, he tells us: "Therefore do not worry, saying, 'What will we eat?' or 'What will we drink?' or 'What will we wear?'" (Matthew 6:31). How could giving Jesus more of your thoughts help you worry less?

4. *Jehovah-Jireh* means that God will provide for all our needs. What are your deepest needs today?

Dear God,
Thank you, Jehovah-Jireh, for providing for
all my needs. Help me to seek your face.

MARY

JANUARY 5

The Arrival

In the time of King Herod, after Jesus was born in Bethlehem of Judea, wise men from the East came to Jerusalem, asking, "Where is the child who has been born king of the Jews? For we observed his star at its rising, and have come to pay him homage." When King Herod heard this, he was frightened, and all Jerusalem with him; and calling together all the chief priests and scribes of the people, he inquired of them where the Messiah was to be born. They told him, "In Bethlehem of Judea; for so it has been written by the prophet:

'And you, Bethlehem, in the land of Judah,
are by no means least among the rulers of Judah;
for from you shall come a ruler
who is to shepherd my people Israel.' "

Then Herod secretly called for the wise men and learned from them the exact time when the star had appeared. Then he sent them to Bethlehem, saying, "Go and search diligently for the child; and when you have found him, bring me word so that I may also go and pay him homage." When they had heard the king, they set out; and there, ahead of them, went the star that they had seen at its rising, until it stopped over the place where the child was. When they saw that the star had stopped, they were overwhelmed with joy. On entering the house, they saw the child with Mary his mother; and they knelt down and paid him homage. Then, opening their treasure chests, they offered him gifts of gold, frankincense, and myrrh. And having been warned in a dream not to return to Herod, they left for their own country by another road.

(Matthew 2:1–12)

●

The Arrival

Our Jehovah-Jireh continues to amaze us with his marvelous provision! Last night as Joseph and I played with Jesus, delighting in his every movement, I heard hooves stomping outside, then voices. Someone knocked.

Joseph rose to answer, and I stretched to see who might be at our door. Darkness would have hidden our visitors, but for the strange, bright star shining over our house, as it had shone above the stable to guide the shepherds the night of Jesus' birth.

This time there were no shepherds. Clothed in robes of rich colors and magnificent designs, these strange men followed Joseph inside. Joy lit their weather-beaten faces. I could only make out pieces of their exuberant explanations. They are "wise men," Magi who study the stars. These Gentiles from the East, no doubt familiar with Daniel's prophecies concerning the "Anointed One," followed the bright star all the way here to worship God's Messiah and Savior.

As soon as the wise men saw Jesus, they knelt and worshiped him. Gentiles who looked like kings knelt before a tiny king. Then they opened their treasure chests and presented Jesus with gifts—not blankets or toys, but gold, frankincense, and myrrh.

I could barely thank them for their generosity, so captivated was I with their story:

"We knew from prophecy that we were searching for the King of the Jews, and so our first stop was in Jerusalem," explained the gray-haired wise man.

His companion interrupted. "We asked in the city streets where we might find the King of the Jews. People eyed us suspiciously and shook their heads. But then—!"

"Tell them about Herod!" urged another visitor.

"Well, the king must have heard about us from many citizens because he summoned us to the palace. He was quite interested in discerning when the star had first appeared."

Another wise man turned to his companions. "Did you notice Herod's countenance when you asked him about the newborn King?"

The other man shook his head. "Herod encouraged us to search in Bethlehem, where his advisors said the Messiah would be born. He told us to return with information so that he too could worship the child."

"But God warned us in a dream not to return to Herod," said the eldest wise man. "We must start our journey home, and we will travel a different route."

PONDERING . . .

1. What do you think the appearance of the wise men meant to Joseph and Mary? How important are the wise men in the account of that first Christmas?

2. January 6 is celebrated as Epiphany, the arrival of the wise men from the East. What helpful reminders can be observed by celebrating the wise men's arrival with much-needed gifts?

3. Most dictionaries define "epiphany" in two ways: a Christian festival held on January 6 in honor of the coming of the three kings to the infant Jesus Christ, and a moment in which you suddenly see or understand something in a new or very clear way. What type of epiphany have you experienced? How did your attitude or actions change because of this "aha" moment?

4. There are many things we aren't told about the wise men in the Scriptures, but we are told enough to celebrate the characteristics they embody: their wisdom, determination, humility, perseverance, and gracious giving. What can you

learn from the wise men? How might you follow the example of these worshipers of Christ?

Dear God,
Blessed be your name
above all names.

MARY

JANUARY 6

Pondering

But Mary treasured all these words and pondered
them in her heart.
(Luke 2:19)

●

Great are the works of the LORD;
studied by all who delight in them.
(Psalm 111:2)

●

Let the one who is wise heed these things
and ponder the loving deeds of the LORD.
(Psalm 107:43, NIV)

●

Now after they [the wise men] had left, an angel of the Lord appeared to Joseph in a dream and said, "Get up, take the child and his mother, and flee to Egypt, and remain there until I tell you; for Herod is about to search for the child, to destroy him." Then Joseph got up, took the child and his mother by night, and went to Egypt, and remained there until the death of Herod. This was to fulfill what had been spoken by the Lord through the prophet, "Out of Egypt I have called my son."

(Matthew 2:13–15)

•

Pondering

Only after the wise men departed did I ponder the gifts they left. I was so overwhelmed with the wise men's generosity, I failed to consider what each gift might mean. The gold will meet all our practical needs, but it is also a symbol of kingship. Jesus is the King of Kings, our royal Ruler.

Frankincense is a fresh incense that, when burned, sends a pleasing aroma to our God in heaven, as do our prayers. Is frankincense not also a symbol of deity and priesthood?

I have puzzled over the gift of myrrh, often more costly than gold. It is part of the anointing oil of a priest, signifying kingship. But myrrh is most often used for burial, a symbol of death. Will not the Messiah live life eternal? In some way, I know these gifts, carried for a thousand miles, speak of the Messiah.

I have been thinking of dear Elizabeth and pondering how lovely and wise she was the instant I arrived on her doorstep. She recognized the Messiah within me at once, as did the child within her.

I was honored by a visit from the angel Gabriel, announcing God's miraculous plan for me and for the world. Joseph, too, had a visit, a dream that this child was sent by God. Later, shepherds received the Good News from a host of angels. And those dear wise men? Their studies led them to a star, and their hearts led them through prophecies to follow that star. Dreams warned them to stay away from Herod on their return home.

Zechariah, Elizabeth's priestly husband, met the angel Gabriel in the temple's Holy Place, where Gabriel revealed to him God's destiny for my son and for his.

But Elizabeth? She is the only one who received neither a visit from an angel, nor a prophetic dream. She was given secondhand information from a man who couldn't speak! Yet she believed, and she received.

I have thought about the holy woman in the temple, Anna the Prophetess. Her joy overflowed as she observed Jesus, as if she'd been waiting her whole life for this moment. How had God prepared her to know and welcome the Messiah? Her arms lifted; but unlike Simeon, Anna turned immediately to other temple-goers and spoke to them of the long-awaited Messiah. "He is now among us!" she declared, for she obviously knew the other faithful worshipers who were awaiting their Savior.

Now, I must pack our belongings and ready for the long journey ahead. Joseph has had another dream. Herod wants to kill Jesus, the one true King, and we are to escape to Egypt. In my heart, I know God will not let Herod succeed. I trust God's perfect plan for his Son and for me. God has promised: "Know that I am with you and will keep you wherever you go, and will bring you back to this land; for I will not leave you until I have done what I have promised you" (Genesis 28:15).

JESUS

In the beginning the Word already existed.
The Word was with God,
and the Word was God.
He existed in the beginning with God.
God created everything through him,
and nothing was created except through him.
The Word gave life to everything that was created,
and his life brought light to everyone.
The light shines in the darkness,
and the darkness can never extinguish it.

(John 1:1–5, NLT)

•

PONDERING . . .
THE THREE WISE WOMEN

Reader, I pray that, in faith, you will join with our sisters in Christ and praise God for the gift of Jesus. Think about Mary, the first wise woman, chosen and blessed by God because she believed that what she was told would come true.

Contemplate dear Elizabeth, the second wise woman, who rejoiced with young Mary, rather than envying her. Let God fill you with shared joy.

Consider the third wise woman, faithful Anna the Prophetess, who was willing to wait in expectation that God would come through on his promises. Like Anna, pass the time in your own waiting room by praising God and sharing the Good News of salvation through Christ.

Think of all Christ went through on earth so we could have our sins forgiven. Praise him for the Resurrection, which made it possible for us to enjoy a relationship with God that will last through eternity.

Then ponder the wonder of Christ in you, the hope of glory.

SCRIPTURE CREDITS

Unless otherwise indicated, Scriptures are taken from the New Revised Standard Version Bible, copyright 1989, Division of Christian Education of the National Council of the Churches of Christ in the United States of America. Used by permission. All rights reserved.

Scripture quotations marked CJB are taken from the Complete Jewish Bible, © 1998 by Messianic Jewish Publishers and Resources. Used by permission.

Scripture quotations marked NASB 1995 are taken from the (NASB®) New American Standard Bible®, Copyright © 1960, 1971, 1977, 1995, by The Lockman Foundation. Used by permission. All rights reserved. www .lockman.org. Scripture quotations marked NASB have the same copyright but add 2020 to the years listed.

Scripture quotations marked NCB are taken from THE NEW CATHOLIC BIBLE®. Copyright © 2019 Catholic Book Publishing Corp. Used by permission. All rights reserved.

Scripture quotations marked NIV are taken from The Holy Bible, New International Version® NIV® Copyright © 1973 1978 1984 2011 by Biblica, Inc.™ Used by permission. All rights reserved worldwide.

Scripture quotations marked NKJV are taken from the New King James Version®. Copyright © 1982 by Thomas Nelson. Used by permission. All rights reserved.

Scripture quotations marked NLT are taken from the Holy Bible, New Living Translation, copyright ©1996, 2004, 2015 by Tyndale House Foundation. Used by permission of Tyndale House Publishers, Carol Stream, Illinois 60188.

Scripture quotations marked RSV are taken from the Revised Standard Version of the Bible, copyright 1952 [2nd edition, 1971] by the Division of Christian Education of the National Council of the Churches of Christ in the United States of America. Used by permission. All rights reserved.

Scripture quotations marked VOICE are taken from taken from The Voice™. Copyright © 2012 by Ecclesia Bible Society. Used by permission. All rights reserved.

FOR FURTHER STUDY

Alpha-Omega Ministries, Inc. *What the Bible Says . . . about The Tabernacle: The Outline Bible Study Series.* Chattanooga, TN: Leadership Ministries Worldwide, 1997.

Burri, Rene. *H. V. Morton in Search of the Holy Land.* New York: Dodd, Mead & Company, Inc, 1979.

Duvall, J. Scott, and J. Daniel Hays, eds. *The Baker Illustrated Bible Background Commentary.* Ada, MI: Baker Books, 2020.

Gower, Ralph. *The New Manners & Customs of Bible Times.* Chicago: Moody Publishers, 2005.

Halley, Henry H. *Halley's Bible Handbook, Classic Edition: Completely Revised and Expanded, by Henry H. Halley.* Grand Rapids, MI: Zondervan, 2014.

Henry, Matthew. *Matthew Henry's Commentary on the Whole Bible*, 6 Volumes. Peabody, MA: Hendrickson Publishers, 2014.

InterVarsity Fellowship. *The Illustrated Bible Dictionary*, 3 Volumes. Downers Grove, IL: InterVarsity Press, 1994.

Jeremias, Joachim. *Jerusalem in the Times of Jesus.* Minneapolis, MN: Fortress, 2014.

Keener, Craig S. *The IVP Bible Background Commentary New Testament.* Downers Grove, IL: InterVarsity Press, 1993.

Rubin, Rabbi Barry, ed. *The Complete Jewish Study Bible: Insights for Jews and Christians.* Peabody, MA: Hendrickson Publishers, 2016.

Strong, James. *The New Strong's Expanded Exhaustive Concordance of the Bible.* Nashville, TN: Thomas Nelson, 2010.

Tenney, Dr. Merrill C. *New Testament Times.* Grand Rapids, MI: Eerdmans, 1965.

Unger, Merrill, revised by Gary N. Larson. *Unger's Bible Handbook.* Chicago: Moody Publishers, 2005.

Wight, Fred H. *Manners & Customs of Bible Lands.* Chicago: Moody Bible Press, 1953.

Young, Robert. *Young's Analytical Concordance to the Bible.* Peabody, MA: Hendrickson Publishers, 2018.

ABOUT THE AUTHOR

Dandi Daley Mackall has spent most of her adult life studying the Bible, leading Bible studies, and writing from a biblical perspective. Her books have won many awards, including the Edgar Award; three Christian Book Awards; Ohio Council International Reading Association Hall of Fame; Amelia Bloom Award for Women; Mom's Choice; NYC Library Top Picks; ALA Best Book. She has received starred reviews from *Publisher's Weekly*, *Booklist*, *Kirkus*, and more, and has been honored to have one of her books become a Hallmark movie. Dandi has written several devotionals for families, novels, children's books and nonfiction offerings including humor and inspiration.

Dandi graduated Magna Cum Laude from the University of Missouri, with a B.A. in foreign languages, later receiving Distinguished Alumna Award. She earned her Master's at University of Central Oklahoma, with the Dean's Art and Achievement Award. Further studies included a year in Hebrew and a year in Greek at Trinity Evangelical Divinity School and courses from the Institute of Biblical Studies. She's taught part-time at Oklahoma University, University of Central Oklahoma, Bethany University, Ashland University in Ohio, Ohio University satellite.

Dandi was a missionary on U.S. college campuses, then became a missionary "behind the Iron Curtain," secretly teaching the Bible to Polish University students, who shared a house with her on the border of Czechoslovakia and Poland.

Currently, Dandi is a national speaker, keynoting at conferences, schools, universities, literary and church events (often about Mary, Elizabeth, and Anna). She's given the Easter address at the Billy Graham Center, the Christmas address at the International Museum of the Bible in Washington, D.C., keynoted at the Association of Christian Schools, the Jennings Foundation, and countless library and literary events. She's made multiple appearances on TV, including ABC, NBC, and CBS, and is a frequent guest on radio shows and podcasts.

Dandi writes from rural Ohio, surrounded by her writer-husband, Joe, their three children and their families, plus horses, dogs, cats, a turtle, a tortoise, a chinchilla, and more.

• • •

Visit Dandi online at www.dandibooks.com.
Follow her on Facebook:
https://www.facebook.com/dandi.mackall

ABOUT PARACLETE PRESS

Paraclete Press is the publishing arm of the Cape Cod Benedictine community, the Community of Jesus. Presenting a full expression of Christian belief and practice, we reflect the ecumenical charism of the Community and its dedication to sacred music, the fine arts, and the written word.

SCAN
TO
READ
MORE

www.paracletepress.com